THE BARONS OF NEWPORT

Statues at Belcourt Castle

By Terrence Gavan

Cover photograph: *The Elms*.
Photo courtesy of Preservation Society of Newport County,
by Richard Cheek

Copyright © 1998 by Terrence Gavan
ISBN 0-929249-06-2

Published by Pineapple Publications
24 Bridge St.
Newport, RI 02840
(401) 847-0859

TABLE OF CONTENTS

INTRODUCTION

They were heady times, those days between 1890 and 1914. It was the Gilded Age, the American Renaissance, and America was develophng a national self-confidence and feeling her oats as an economic and political world power. It was a time of opportunity, tremendous opportunity, particularly for accumulating wealth, as the federal income tax and anti-trust laws were a thing of the future.

Americans were gathering wealth at a frightening pace. In the middle of the 19th century there were only a few millionaires, but by the turn of the century there were a few thousand.

Much of this new wealth gravitated to Newport, Rhode Island, and the City by the Sea became the principal watering hole for a new class of aristocrats.

The Barons of Newport reveals the behavior of this remarkable group and illustrates the results of a lifestyle uninhibited by financial constraints.

In this story you'll meet a most incredible cast of characters, including the world's richest families: the Vanderbilts and the Astors. You'll follow prominent members of the elite and exalted Four Hundred, see their outrageous and extravagant lifestyles, and walk through their wondrous summer mansions.

As you read about the fabulous fortunes of the barons of Newport, it's important to note that their wealth was denominated in the turn-of-the-century dollar, a currency much more valuable than today's dollar. The equivalent buying power of a dollar in 1900 was several times greater than a dollar today. So a Gilded Age millionaire would be equal to today's multi-millionaire.

Most of the family dynasties of the Gilded Age have long since dispersed or withered, but most of Gilded Age Newport has been preserved. You can still view and even tour the fabulous mansions. You can stroll Cliff Walk and Bellevue Avenue, visit the Casino, and drive Ocean Drive (but you still can't get into Bailey's Beach). This book will help you plan your tour, find your way around, and I hope, give you a sense of a society of extravagance and ostentation that will never be duplicated.

Terrence Gavan
Newport, Rhode Island

NEWPORT

The American Capital of Conspicuous Consumption

At the turn of the century, Newport was the social pinnacle, the epitome, the hands-down Mecca. Sure there were formidable pretenders–Palm Beach, Bar Harbor, Saratoga–but none could compare.

There were few doubters; Newport Rhode Island reigned supreme as the queen of American resorts from 1890 to 1914 (the Gilded Age). During these glory days the absolute upper crust made Newport its summer headquarters. Newport was simply the place to be.

American society catapulted to world prominence during this era, and European royalty flocked to Newport to rub elbows with the social titans and fortune hunt among their debutantes.

This era saw the genesis of the American woman as a social and political force, and this force was ratified by the suffragette movement. The deep pockets and strong will of Newport's Alva Vanderbilt Belmont were formidable ammunition in this struggle. She contributed heavily to the movement and sponsored a suffragette rally at her Bellevue Avenue mansion, Marble House. The emerging power of women was clearly evident in Newport society, and in more than just the suffragette movement.

Although men made the money and built industrial empires, it was women who defined the new American social phenomenon of conspicuous consumption. In most cases the men were willing collaborators, but they generally lacked the time, talent, or interest in the daily minutia society demanded.

Gilded Age women of wealth, lacking the cultural license to engage in industrial empire building, were relegated by default to running households and filling time as they saw fit. So, they took what freedoms they had and parlayed them into a social juggernaut of extravagance and opulence. They created society with a capital "S" and in the process controlled immense power and wealth. Newport was the arena for their social conflicts, the catalyst for their extravagance, and the setting for their marriage brokering.

The dowagers and matrons of Newport had virtual *carte blanche* in the daily operation of their households (which they often ruled with an iron hand) and in the financing of their lavish and innovative affairs.

As much as men, if not more, women were the "Barons of Newport," and in this book, "Barons" is a genderless term.

EARLY PROSPERITY

Newport was famous on its own account long before the dawn of the Gilded Age.

A group of religious dissidents from the Massachusetts Bay Colony founded Newport in 1639. The progenitors of many eminent Newport families were in this group: Coddington, Easton, Coggeshall, Brenton, and Hazard. Through the industriousness and vision of these early colonists, Newport quickly achieved economic prominence and, during the early 1700s, ranked equally with New York, Boston, and Philadelphia.

Throughout the first half of the 1700s, the seaport flourished as an export center for shipbuilding, farming, and manufacturing of fine furniture and silverware. Newport became a supplier to other coastal colonies as well as the West Indies and Europe. The port city played a key role in the illicit but profitable "triangle trade," which involved exchanging rum, molasses, and slaves between New England, the West Indies, and Africa. Many prominent merchants were engaged in the slave trade–a principal contributor to the growth of Newport's affluence.

Newport Waterfront, c. 1900

5

CULTURAL MAGNET

Increased prosperity fostered development of the arts and trades. Architecture and carpentry thrived on the need for public buildings and homes for the affluent.

Many prominent travelers visited colonial Newport, and it became a principal gateway between the old and new worlds. Some of these visitors settled in the city and greatly enhanced the cultural atmosphere. George Berkeley, a powerful figure in religion and literature, spent several years in Newport before returning to England.

An atmosphere of religious tolerance promoted the immigration of many persecuted minorities. Most notable were Quakers, Jews, and Baptists. The spirit of cooperation and diligence of these people contributed much to the city's economy. It also helped create a cultural center and a cosmopolitan society unrivaled in the New World.

Colonial Newport became a thriving tourist center. Summer visitors came from up and down the east coast and as far away as the Caribbean. Because of its strong maritime trade, Newport had a widespread reputation. The island was known for its healthful air and climate. Visitors from the south mixed well and had much in common with the agriculture and merchant families of Newport.

Newport is the best living example of American Colonial heritage. The City by the Sea probably has more original Colonial houses still standing than anywhere. Newport is famous for the oldest American synagogue (Touro), the oldest library (Redwood), and the first tavern (White Horse).

THE REVOLUTION

Colonial Newport's affluence and wealth soon attracted the attention of the British government. Perhaps it was greed, envy, or an exhausted treasury (the financial results of numerous wars with France and Spain), but the "mother" country began enforcing restrictive trade and maritime tax laws.

This led to several incidents during the late 1760s between the British Navy and Colonial rebels. Colonists burned customs ships in and around Newport harbor, and riots were widespread. The city population divided between loyalist and patriot.

The low point of Newport's history was a three-year period beginning in December 1776 when a British fleet landed with a force of 6,000 troops. The tyrannical General Prescott commanded the British occupation force and made life as wretched as possible for the colonists who remained in Newport. Many prominent families, their lives in ruin, fled the city. Eventually, the British ended their occupation upon news of an approaching French force. However, before their departure, the British looted the city, burned houses and wharves, and cut down nearly all the trees. This destroyed the economic vitality and cultural spirit of an already demoralized population. Newporters survived the approaching cold winter by ripping firewood from abandoned houses.

A mild renaissance occurred during the ensuing French occupation and restored much of the lost spirit and gaiety to Newport's soul. The gallant French officers led by General Rochambeau won the hearts of the people.

General George Washington met Rochambeau in Newport to plan the decisive battle of Yorktown.

TRANSITION PERIOD

After the revolution Newport never again emerged as a dominant commercial force. Continuous maritime hostilities with England made trading difficult, as Newport was practically cut out of markets in the Caribbean. Later, with the advent of the railroad, the importance of maritime trade waned, and Newport's island isolation left it cut off from any land routes.

There was little activity in Newport during the early 1800s Newporter Oliver Perry was famous in the War of 1812 for "meeting the enemy" during the Battle of Lake Erie, and his brother Matthew Perry helped open trade with Japan. The Perrys were part of the roots of the rich naval tradition found hn Newport.

By the middle of the 19th century, summer visitors began to trickle back into Newport. Slowly the city regained prominence as a tourist center. Hotels and inns flourished as resorters flocked to enjoy the healthful air and mild climate. But the advent of the Civil War abruptly ended a budding summer migration of southern gentry, mostly wealthy planters.

After the war, a large and diverse group of New England intellectuals made Newport their summer retreat and served to renew the city's moribund cultural heritage.

Luminaries like Oliver Wendell Holmes, Henry Wadsworth Longfellow,

Henry and William James, Edith Wharton, Julia Ward Howe, John Singer Sargent, John LaFarge, and Edgar Allen Poe (one season) summered in Newport. Even Bret Harte livened several dinner parties during the summer of 1871.

This cultural cream, along with other wealthy Boston Brahmins, built stately but tasteful cottages, mostly on the hill near the center of the city. The area along lower Bellevue Avenue and Ochre Point was as yet only sparsely developed.

GILDED AGE

Suddenly the scene shifted. Late in the nineteenth century, Gilded Age millionaires, attracted by Newport's cultural reputation and the opportunity to mingle with the intelligentsia, descended in droves on the City by the Sea.

The elite (but snobbish in their own way) intellectuals wanted no part of this gaudy *noveau riche* group. So, the intellectuals vacated Newport, inadvertently driven out by the new social invaders, and from then on, distinguished party guests like Bret Harte would be replaced by the likes of an Austrian archduke or an English polo champion.

Who were these people, where did they come from, and how did they get so rich? Well, they were the Vanderbilts, the Astors, the Belmonts, the Fishes, the Havemeyers, the Goelets, the Berwinds, and hundreds more. They came from all over the country, but mostly from New York.

They got so rich by benefiting enormously from several phenomena like the Industrial Revolution, the Civil War (profiteering), lack of a federal income tax, abundant and cheap immigrant labor, and a combination of creativity and hard work with a dash of ruthlessness.

These *noveau riche* with their sudden wealth often lacked the polish and grace required for aristocratic status. Their collective insecurity, supplemented by a restlessness for recognition, contributed greatly to the excesses of their lifestyles. So, when they needed a summer retreat as a depository for their ostentation, they looked to Newport with its colonial heritage and understated patrician demeanor.

These Gilded Agers left an indelible imprint on the City by the Sea, as attested by their monumental mansions (some seemingly a cross between Grand Central Station and the Palace of Versailles).

Criticisms of this group ranged from silly, to scandalous, to insensi-

The Breakers, c. 1900

tive, to immoral. Across the country, from editorial pages to pulpits, editors and preachers railed against them. The budget for one of their balls or their summer wardrobe could feed hordes or starving poor. The example set by this class came under constant attack. This group through its lifestyle was accused of many sins but, as we shall see, one of them was not dullness.

The Newport invasion was led by the pioneering August Belmonts. As a member of the Rothschild family, August Belmont Senior was gilded with European banking money, and his wife Caroline was the daughter of Commodore Matthew Perry. Their mansion, By-the-Sea, was one of the first along Bellevue Avenue. The Belmonts began throwing lavish parties and parading up Bellevue Avenue in their French carriage. The Old Guard was offended by such exhibition, but their protests were futile as the floodgates opened before a rush of Astors, Vanderbilts, Van Rensselaers, and Stuyvesants. The Belmonts proved to be bellwethers.

Thus began the Gilded Age of Newport, the splendor of which the world has rarely seen. The summer colonists built their lavish mansions (always called cottages no matter what their size or cost) along Bellevue Avenue and around Ochre Point and Ocean Drive.

Newport became the Mecca for high society and a playground for the new American aristocrats.

OF MANSIONS AND MADNESS

So, the Gilded Agers made Newport their summer Mecca, and the race was on. Competition for position in the social order was intense. Even Old Line New York families like the Van Alens and the Goelets found themselves drawn into the fray as the struggle of upmanship expanded.

Of course financial strength and genealogy played a role in social standing, but as the Gilded Age developed, other factors rose to prominence. The size, grandeur, and location of one's cottage was critical, and other issues such as lavish balls, expensive wardrobes, and fancy yachts were important.

COTTAGES AND KINGS

The Cottagers chose Bellevue Avenue, Ochre Point, and Ocean Drive as the stage for their exhibitionism. Here they built a most magnificent and monumental collection of private residences. All sorts of architectural styles were represented, ranging from stately Victorian manor houses, to Italian renaissance villas, to French chateaus, to English castles.

Richard Morris Hunt and Stanford White were the premier architects of the Gilded Age. Although they both designed a series of stately and

Rosecliff, c. 1900

tasteful Newport cottages (particularly White), they also contributed greatly (particularly Hunt) to the collection of magnificent stone palaces that are so dominant. Architectural purists have called these creations absurd white elephants and condemned the designers for their corruption. Nevertheless, Hunt and White were prolific and powerful forces in the gilded culture.

Stanford White of the New York architectural firm of McKim, Mead and White was the creator of Tessie Oelrich's Rosecliff, Mamie Fish's Crossways, Edwin Morgan's Beacon Rock, the famed Newport Casino, and several other elegant shingle-style cottages. However, it was Richard Morris Hunt who had the most profound impact on the architecture of the time.

Educated at the Beaux Arts school in Paris, where he embraced the "classic" style of architecture, Hunt translated his training to the United States and led the so-called American Renaissance revolution in architecture. The timing was right, as Hunt's bent toward the classic European style of architecture matched with the unlimited wealth and the burning desire for ostentation of the Gilded Agers.

Hunt became the architect-in-residence for the Vanderbilts, the Belmonts, and the Goelets and designed the most famous Newport mansions: The Breakers (Cornelius Vanderbilt), Marble House (William K. Vanderbilt), Belcourt Castle (O.H.P. Belmont), and Ochre Court (Ogden Goelet). He also designed no less than George Washington Vanderbilt's mind-boggling Biltmore estate in the North Carolina mountains and William K. Vanderbilt's imposing French chateau on Fifth Avenue.

THE SOCIAL GATEKEEPER

For two months each summer the social invasion was in full force. In its early stages, Newport society was shaped by one Ward McAllister, the developer of the famous list of four hundred. Mister Make-a-Lister, as he was called, asserted that there were only "about four hundred people in fashionable New York society. If you go outside that number you strike people who are either not at ease in a ballroom or make other people not at ease."

McAllister was a southern lawyer with roots in Newport as an early summer colonist. He bought a Newport farm and threw many popular picnics. McAllister was an expert at party planning, a master of pomposity and snob, *par excellence*. He filled a vacuum in a rapidly developing so-

11

cial world by becoming its arbiter. He soon latched on to Mrs. Caroline Astor, a prime mover who made him the gatekeeper of society.

When McAllister died in 1895, he was succeeded by the even more bizarre and certainly more interesting, Harry Lehr.

BALLS AND DINNERS

The balls and dinner parties of Newport society were unmatched and would surely rival those from any previous era.

The Pembroke Joneses from North Carolina earmarked $300,000 for entertaining during each Newport season. A single Newport ball could cost as much as $200,000. Mrs. Elbridge Gerry and Mrs. Ogden Mills claimed that they could throw a party for a hundred without adding to their servant staff.

This was Newport at its social apex; ten-course meals with solid gold services were par for the course.

Mrs. Stuyvesant Fish

At the infamous "Dogs Dinner", sponsored by Elizabeth Drexel Lehr and Mamie Fish, a hundred dogs feasted on stewed liver, rice, and fricassee of bones. It took the twisted mind of Harry Lehr to concoct such an unusual event that featured all manner of society's canines, some appropriately dressed for the occasion, dining on the verandah of the Lehr cottage. The "Dogs Dinner," occurring during the mid-1890s depression, gained national publicity and rebuke from the pulpits and editorial pages.

Costume balls were common in Newport, and they reached great heights of innovation. At Mamie Fish's Mother Goose Ball in 1913, 200 guests

*Mrs. Stuart Duncan
at the Mother Goose Ball, 1913*

were attired in costumes based on Mother Goose nursery rhymes, and her Crossways mansion was fully decked in Mother Goose motif.

Henry Clews, Jr., the Wall Street brokerage heir, held a parodical Servants' Ball. Guests were invited to dress as the servant of their choice. It was a ball that didn't amuse the servant corps. Guests arrived to witness a Harry Lehr greeting as butler, Tessie Oelrichs moping the floor, and O.H.P. Belmont taking cloaks.

One costume ball prompted a fitting malapropism from a bewildered footman when he announced a diminutive Henry Carter dressed as Henry IV and his rotund wife dressed as a Norman peasant. The confused footman's announcement was loud and clear: "Henry IV and an enormous pheasant."

Rosecliff was the setting for some of Newport's most memorable balls (and it still is). For the White Ball, Tessie Oelrich's elegant terra-cotta chateau was decked entirely in white, and guests wore nothing but white. Revelers could look out from the country's largest ballroom and view a veritable fleet of full sized model ships, with their white sails billowing, decorating the back lawn .

The height of decadence, in the eyes of many, was the famous Monkey Dinner. In another creation from the contorted mind of Harry Lehr, and in collusion with Mamie Fish, a monkey in full formal dress was the surprise guest of honor at Lehr's mansion. Guests were invited to meet Prince del Drago, a Corsican nobleman, but what they got was a tuxedoed monkey who behaved rather well during dinner, but took to the chandeliers and began throwing lightbulbs after the champagne caught up with him. It was all hilariously amusing for the guests, but a collective gasp could almost be heard from the old line Newporters, and of course the newspapers had a field day.

RULES AND RITUALS

In the early part of the Gilded Age, when Mrs. Astor was in firm control, it was much more difficult for wealthy upstarts to penetrate society's barriers. Mrs. Astor insisted that candidates for the exalted circle be cleansed of the effects of working in trade. It usually took two generations for the money to cool off. Later these standards didn't hold up and were replaced by more subjective and political criteria.

But you didn't enter Newport society in one year, no matter who you were. If you were an aspiring social gate crasher, you'd be advised to move gradually. First you may want to spend a season in Bar Harbor, get to know some of the right people. Then if you go to Newport, don't buy a cottage, maybe just rent one. If you can, find a patron, a supporter from the upper echelons of the Four Hundred. Try to get invited to an important party. And if you do, don't try to out-dress, out-jewel, or out-entertain any of the established socialites. This would be the kiss of death. And remember, when you're out in your coach on Bellevue Avenue for an afternoon drive, don't ever overtake a woman of higher social standing.

Exchanging calling cards was an unusual ritual peculiar to Gilded Age society. Most summer afternoons, the family, dressed to the nines, boarded their shiny coach, driven by liveried coachmen decked in family colors (maroon for Vanderbilts and blue for Astors), to call on other women of equal caste. At this point, the men would try to repair to the Reading Room or their yacht.

A stroll down Bellevue Avenue

Strangely, the visitors never entered their neighbor's cottage, but if they did, the mistress would have been out in her coach visiting other neighbors. Callers merely sent their footman in to leave a calling card with the neighbor's footman. This could consume a great part of the afternoon.

This puzzling affair was extremely formal and often preceded a full-blown coaching parade along Bellevue Avenue and around Ocean Drive. Victorias, phaetons, four-in-hands, and all manner of shiny black coaches participated in the exhibition. Stiff-backed and poker-faced, the coachmen ritualistically drove the ten-mile route, while the matrons solemnly bowed to one another in cult-like recognition.

The constraints on members of the privileged class could be smothering, particularly on the children. Girls were especially affected.

In Consuelo Vanderbilt's memoirs, she complains about her morning attire, which consisted of a floor-length dress with a high and tight whalebone collar and a corset strangling her waist to the prescribed eighteen inches. Her huge hat was festooned with flowers and feathers and held to her hair with long steel pins. A veil hid her face, and tight gloves squeezed her hands. All she needed was her parasol, and she was off to Bailey's Beach for her morning dip!

Wearing her dark dress and black stockings, she bobbed in the waves, protected from the sun by her large hat.

Consuelo Vanderbilt,
the Duchess of Marlborough

Consuelo abhorred the daily tedium which included no sports like tennis or golf, but instead, finishing-school type lessons in deportment and etiquette. She was constantly controlled and censored by her governess and her mother.

When it came to marriage, the control was highly evident, particularly in Consuelo's case. She was the victim of a bitter brokered marriage to the Duke of Marlborough, which eventually ended in divorce.

The rules of chaperonage in the Gilded Age were peculiar. It seems that a young lady could not go alone to the theater with a gentleman unless they were engaged. However, she could ride with him all day, and the couple could sit down alone together on any isolated hilltop they could find.

MARRIAGE NEWPORT STYLE

In Newport, marriage brokering was extensive, and not surprisingly, so was divorce. Many of the Vanderbilts and most of the Astors (particularly the later generations) were divorced. John Jacob Astor VI's marital affairs were so complicated that he petitioned the New York court to decide which woman was his wife, and Cornelius Vanderbilt IV was married seven times.

Automobile magnate William Budlong was sued for divorce twenty-one times. On several occasions, Mrs. Budlong exiled him from their mansion, and he was relegated to morning entreaties before her bedroom window in order to get a clean shirt. Eventually they were divorced for good.

Since many of these marriages were not founded on love, infidelity was not unusual. In Cornelius Vanderbilt IV's memoirs he describes his mother discussing this issue with his aunt, May Goelet, on the lawn of her mansion, Ochre Court. "Of course he has a mistress," was the nonchalant remark.

In her autobiography, Blanche Oelrichs describes illicit trysts in the woods near Hanging Rock overlooking Sachuest Beach.

BACKSTAIRS

The servant staff, obviously the backbone of mansion operations, was stratified into a highly structured caste system. Everyone knew their place in this social microcosm. The butler and chief chef were of the highest rank, and personal maids and valets were much higher in status than footmen, stable boys, or upstairs maids. A butler would not serve dinner or empty ashtrays, he may not even answer the door. A woman's personal maid would not make a bed or clean the bedroom.

In addition to the butlers, chefs, maids, valets, stableboys, and footman, there were coachman, nannies, governesses, social secretaries, gardeners, and yacht crews. This group often performed Herculean feats that were largely unrecognized. This often related to planning and executing enormously complex dinners, parties, or balls with little advance warning.

Azar, O.H.P Belmont's Arabian valet, was a colorful character around Belcourt Castle. With his flashy military jacket and red fez, he attentively stood behind Belmont's enormous armchair as guests were greeted in the Grand Hall at Belcourt. After Belmont promoted him to chief butler, Azar would dazzle guests in uniforms glittering with gold. He exuded an overwhelming aura of grandeur and superiority, as he stood between two English footmen in full livery and powered hair, and greeted guests with ultimate pomp and circumstance.

Morton, Mamie Fish's butler was the model of impassiveness. He awed even his employers with his haughtiness and unruffled superiority. After all, he had served English royalty. However, one day after a tiff with Mrs. Fish over an unusual number of luncheon guests, he was fired. In revenge, he disassembled all of her gold dinner service the night before a large dinner party at Crossways.

The servants generally got little respect and even less salary, but in those days there were plenty of them available–such that Perry Belmont could station a footman holding a candelabrum on every sixth step of the Belcourt Castle stairway.

Even well known professional entertainers were treated as second class to the Four Hundred. When Mrs. Cornelius Vanderbilt engaged violinist Fritz Kreisler to play at one of her dinner parties, he quoted her a fee of thirteen thousand dollars. Without a blink she agreed, but then asked him not to mix with her guests after the performance. Then with a masterful rejoinder, Kreisler quickly responded, "In that case, my fee is only five hundred."

Bonniecrest, Mr. and Mrs. Stuart Duncan

THE GILDED PLAYGROUND

In the late 1800s, leisure time activities began to flourish. The prosperity at the dawn of the Gilded Age spawned several gentleman sports, and this was nowhere more evident than in Newport, where golf, tennis, polo, yachting, coaching, and automobiling were integral elements of an emerging society.

Of course, Newport became famous as the home of the America's Cup for more than fifty years. The Newport Country Club was the scene of the first US Open golf championship. The Newport Casino hosted the first national tennis championship in 1881, and is currently the home of the Tennis Hall of Fame. And so on.

The automobile was common in turn-of-the-century Newport. Resorters called them "bubbles," and considered them a novelty. Still, Newport is credited with promoting the automobile craze, for people all over wanted what Newport society had.

America's first automobile race was run on Sachuest Beach, as steamers, electrics, and internal combustion contraptions–manned by queer looking drivers decked in dusters, goggles, long gauntlet gloves, and caps with huge visors–chugged whirled and jerked down the two-mile course at twenty miles per hour.

It never dawned on the cottagers that automobiles would be anything more than a passing fancy. Stuyvesant Fish would later recall "Nobody dreamed that automobiles would come into general use."

On the other hand, the shiny black horse-drawn coaches were much more popular, and elaborate coaching parades along Bellevue Avenue were highlights of a summer season.

The love affair with horses was extensive and highly developed. The horses lived the good life in enormous stone stables along Coggeshall Avenue, one block below Bellevue.

In the late 1800s, the rapidly emerging wealthy class was growing in power and wealth and in the process established various institutions of leisure to enhance its gaiety. Private clubs and societies of exclusivity appeared. One of the most notable being the Newport Casino, America's first country club.

THE CASINO AND THE COMMODORE

The Newport Casino was the brainchild of James Gordon Bennett, Jr., an overbearing iconoclast who was a publishing and yachting pioneer. Bennett was truly a driven man and created the Casino out of spite for the Newport establishment.

Bennett was the publisher of the New York Herald and the Paris Herald, and he was also famous for sending Stanley into Africa to find Livingstone. He was a yachtsman extraordinaire and was a commodore of the New York Yacht Club. Bennett was a flamboyant big spender who easily went through thirty million dollars on his various whimsical projects.

The man could likely be reincarnated in today's Ted Turner, the famous broadcast magnate and America's Cup skipper who has paralleled Bennett's lifestyle and accomplishments in so many ways.

It seems that Bennett, an early Newport resorter, was in a rowdy mood one day when he challenged his friend, Captain "Sugar" Candy, a British lancer and polo player, to gallop his horse across the porch of the venerable Newport Reading Room. Candy accepted the challenge and charged up the stairs and into the hall, routing the astonished clubmen.

The Board of Governors of the Reading Room censured Bennett and withdrew Captain Candy's guest invitation. A relatively mild admonishment it was, but enough to enrage Bennett who felt he had *carte blanche* in Newport.

Anyway, Bennett decided to supplant the stodgy Reading Room with a modern country club that would include lawn tennis courts, card rooms, a theater, and a restaurant. So, he hired the prominent architect Stanford White to create a most elegant complex.

Despite Bennett's imperious manner, he gave White a free hand in designing the Casino. The block-long complex was built on upper Bellevue Avenue.

Bellevue Avenue near the Casino

The clubhouse combined Victorian charm with Chinese detail. Its shingled exterior and multi-gabled roof line surrounded a picturesque courtyard with a clock tower, horseshoe piazza, and several latticed porches. Mullaly's String Orchestra played on the piazza each morning, while club members gossiped from the second floor terrace.

The Casino opened in 1880, and in 1881, it hosted the first national tennis championship, the United States Lawn Tennis Tournament. The tournament remained at the Casino until 1915, when it moved to Forest Hills, New York (it's now called the US Open and is at Flushing, New York).

In those days only bluebloods played in tournaments, and Boston Brahmin Richard Sears, decked in knickers, with wool socks, blazer, cap, and rubber-soled canvas shoes, won the championship eight years in a row.

Tennis Week was a social highlight every August as Newport's elite displayed themselves to each other in the highest of fashion. Grandstand seats were status symbols granted by birthright to the cream of American society. Of course, every year the same seats went to the Vanderbilts, the Astors, the Belmonts, and the Goelets.

With its social, theatrical, and athletic activities, the Casino became the cultural center of Newport. The tennis games, concerts, and dances were widely attended.

The Casino helped usher in a new era of social life. It was the Gay Nineties, formality and lavish entertainment were coming into vogue, and balls and banquets were replacing intimate dinners and high teas.

THE YACHTING CAPITAL OF THE WORLD

Pleasure yachting on a grand scale got its start in Newport. The early yachts of the Gilded Age were truly magnificent and costly.

Only the highest strata of society could afford such extravagant luxuries. The Vanderbilt yachts were legendary for their luxurious accommodations and sheer size. At 285 feet, William K. Vanderbilt's *Alva* was the largest and most expensive yacht of its time (1886). After *Alva* sank, Willie K. replaced her with the even larger, *Valiant*, and later Cornelius Vanderbilt III, himself a commodore of the New York Yacht Club, built the steam yacht *North Star*, one of the largest of its time.

During this golden age of the private yacht, Newport Harbor was the summer anchorage for such fabulous vessels as JP Morgan's *Corsair,* with its crew of eighty-five; James Gordon Bennett's steam yacht *Lysistrata*;

the Astor's *Nourmahal*; the Drexel's *Sultana*; the Leed's *Noma*; and the Widener's *Josephine*. Mrs. Richard Cadwalader's 407-foot *Savarona* was too large for the harbor, and the world's largest yacht, sporting a full-sized pipe organ and decked with Persian rugs and tapestries, had to anchor out in Narragansett Bay.

Bennett's *Lysistrata* sailed the world and was equipped with a Turkish bath and a miniature dairy. The unpredictable Bennett once absconded with three prominent women (including a countess and a lady) during a dinner party for them aboard his yacht in Newport harbor. After quaffing generous amounts of champagne, Bennett ordered the yacht to sea and promptly passed out in his cabin. When the ladies pleaded with the first officer to return to Newport, he simply stated that he had orders from the Commodore to sail for Egypt. They had to wait until morning when the Commodore awoke and agreed to return home.

Although Newport hosted several important yacht races each summer, in 1930, the America's Cup series arrived (with its magnificent J-boats), and the City by the Sea was officially sanctified as the yachting capital of the world.

LIFE WAS A BEACH

As a beach, it was no big deal (Newport had several that were much better); nevertheless, Bailey's was the ultimate beach. Bailey's Beach was

Bailey's Beach, c. 1930

21

a postage stamp of sand and seaweed at the southern end of Bellevue Avenue. Modest in size, the Spouting Rock Beach Association (its formal name) was probably the most difficult (and therefore the most sought after) private club to join in all of American society.

A resorter may make it into the Casino, the Clambake Club, or even the Reading Room, but Bailey's Beach was always the toughest. Its exclusivity was even more pronounced because its facilities were so limited. There were only eighty-one outside cabanas.

Protocol was strictly enforced, no transgressions were permitted; bathers had to be covered from head to toe. Bathing at Bailey's was a full-dress affair.

Bailey's was far from luxurious, dressing rooms were simple wooden cubicles. Its cachet was its clientele. They were the *creme de la creme*, and membership was the greatest social merit badge.

The Bailey's "bathing suit" was a far cry from today's bikini. Proper Newport society would be a laughing stock by modern standards. The women would be exceptionally hilarious in their standard-issue black regalia. Long black skirts over heavy black pantaloons and black stockings were common. Some even wore awkward black bathing shoes. One day, tremors went up and down Bellevue Avenue when Mrs. Herbert Parsons dared to appear without the prescribed black stockings.

The men could be a bit eccentric too. Herman Oelrichs would float for hours fully loaded with picnic pail, whiskey flask, cigar box, and a stack of books, and James Van Alen usually bathed with his monocle, straw hat, and cigar.

THE HORSEY SET

On the surface, it seemed mild enough: pedigreed horses pulling elegant black coaches in a parade along Bellevue Avenue.

But there was another side to the sport of coaching, and James Gordon Bennett, Jr. was its principal promoter. Bennett was a speed merchant; he loved to race and not just in organized races. He would fly down country roads driving at breakneck speeds, sometimes in the middle of the night. Often after a few drinks, he would take reckless midnight rides, driving naked in the coach box. "I want to be able to breathe," he explained.

In one incident, Bennett nearly affected the outcome of history when he went on a wild coaching ride with Jennie Jerome, the future mother of

Mr. and Mrs. Alfred Vanderbilt after a coaching victory

Winston Churchill. They were nearly killed when Bennett flipped the coach while careening around a corner.

Bennett and some of the Belmont clique (Leonard Jerome, August Belmont, William Travers, and Henry Clews) introduced coaching to Newport.

In addition to coach racing, coaching parades were highly popular. An entire subculture and jargon developed around the sport. Form and dress were important ingredients. A "whip" was a coaching aficionado who observed proper protocol while driving. He would be decked in a vivid green topcoat with boutonniere, a yellow-striped waistcoat, silk top hat, and shiny patent-leather boots. A "whip" could become a "howling swell" by attaching a bunch of flowers to the neck of each horse.

This more serene side of coaching was really an exhibition of one's wealth and status. During the Gay Nineties, all manner of tiny phaetons, low victorias, elegant landau's, convertible barouches, and four-in-hands could be seen clattering along Bellevue Avenue, with tooting horns, cracking whips, and jingling chains. The equipment was fancy, and everything gleamed with polish and wax, from the coachmen's boots to the horses' hides.

The unique August Belmont coach was drawn by four horses, the lead two mounted by postillions dressed as jockeys.

The formal parade was a daily highlight along Bellevue Avenue, but the stiffness and aloofness of the participants would make it seem a bizarre ritual by today's standards. The horses, the central figures of the show, were highly trained steeds. The high-stepping "leaders" were like seasoned actors haughtily tossing their heads, while the "wheelers" kept their hoofs low to the ground, anchoring the team.

Elsie French Vanderbilt and E.J. Berwind at Newport Polo

August Belmont was considered a great reinsman, and his horses "Rockingham" and "Waltzingham" were classic high-steppers. Alfred Vanderbilt drove a great duo in "Schoolgirl" and "Lady Teazle." Reggie Vanderbilt's horses, hailing from Sandy Point Farm, may have been the best in Newport; he won several prizes with his favorite horse "Doctor Schwonk." Pierre Lorillard's "Parole" won purses of $118,000, an astronomical sum at that time.

Horses were treated royally in their huge stone stables, their every need attended to by a retinue of stable hands. O.H.P. Belmont couldn't bear to be too far from his horses, so his were lodged on the first floor of Belcourt Castle. Richard Morris Hunt, the architect of the Breakers, designed their stalls. Belmont gave them changes of equipment three times a day and provided gold-embroidered white linen sheets for their bed. Belmont loved his horses so much that he had his two favorites stuffed and mounted on the second floor of Belcourt.

Mrs. Alva Vanderbilt Belmont had two saddles, one for riding left, the other for riding right, which she alternated regularly to protect her figure from distortion.

The annual September horse show at the Casino was well attended by the barons of Newport, segregated from the commoners in their exclusive hundred dollar boxes.

MRS. ASTOR

The Queen of Newport

She was known simply as Mrs. Astor. But she was the mistress of Beechwood, Newport's first queen, and the high priestess of American society.

Caroline Schermerhorn Astor was the ruler of the Four Hundred and the trailblazer for an emerging aristocratic class. In collaboration with her prime minister, Ward McAllister, she built American society on a grand scale, established its rules and rituals, and decided who belonged and who didn't. Jews, Irish, and most Catholics were generally excluded.

In the early days, Mrs. Astor had near dictatorial powers over her class. People likened her to Queen Victoria; she dressed the part and acted the part. She was like a cult figure; everyone paid homage. The recognition she bestowed upon an aspiring social climber usually meant the difference between high society membership and social oblivion.

Mrs. Astor raised jewel wearing to a high plateau of ostentation. She never wore jewelry during the day, but at night she became a dazzling spectacle in her trademark diamond tiara, a stunning diamond stomacher, a triple-stranded diamond necklace (204 stones), and various chains of diamonds dispersed about her person. Also, her fingers were filled with rings of diamonds and other precious stones

According to Mrs. Astor's dictum, it took three generations of wealth untainted by work "in trade" to qualify for social acceptability. The money had to "cool off," as she

The Mrs. Astor

put it. Conveniently, Mrs., Astor's husband was the grandson of *The* John Jacob Astor I, and the Astor fortune was invested in real estate, an acceptable pursuit. Not just money, but lineage was also essential for entre to the rarefied air of high society. Mrs. Astor's pedigree traced back to New York Dutch aristocracy of the Knickerbocker period.

However, the Vanderbilts in spite of their millions, still worked in the railroads and therefore, didn't exist in Mrs. Astor's world. Of course, this all changed when the formidable Alva Vanderbilt extorted Mrs. Astor's imprimatur when Alva agreed to invite her debutante daughter to an absolutely critical coming-out ball.

Physically, Mrs. Astor appeared an unlikely candidate for her exalted stature, she was far from beautiful and looked somewhat dumpy with her short stature, large jaw, and prominent nose.

Mrs. Astor's husband, William Backhouse Astor, Jr., was a rather dour gentleman who lacked the refinement and ambition to accompany his wife on her social adventures. William was much more concerned with horse breeding, yachting, and womanizing–not necessarily in that order. Parties aboard his sailing yacht, *Ambassadress* or his steam yacht, *Nourmahal* usually included a multitude of unescorted women; they never included Mrs. Astor.

William's grandfather, John Jacob Astor, the founder of the family fortune, was an illiterate German immigrant who came to America in 1784 with $25 in his pocket. He became interested in the fur business and rapidly rose from simple fur trader to monopolist over the American market. As his fur business expanded, he invested the profits in real estate, and by 1835 he was the richest man in the world. Eventually, the Astor family real estate holdings became so extensive that the Astors were known as the landlords of New York City. John Jacob left his son, William Backhouse Astor, an estate valued at $40 million. William doubled his inheritance and left $80 million to be divided between his two sons, John Jacob Astor III and William Backhouse Astor, Jr. (Mrs. Astor's husband).

With the Astor millions behind her, Mrs. Astor was heavily armed for her ascendancy. In the early 1870s, the Astor's Fifth Avenue mansion was the seat of social power, as Mrs. Astor began collaborating with Ward McAllister to set the standards and establish the caste system that would govern society. Her annual New York ball was the pinnacle of each social season. An invitation was prized by every socialite, since it ratified her elite status. After dinner and before dancing, Mrs. Astor would hold court from a long couch (appropriately known as the throne), receiving visitors she personally selected for special attention. This practice identified her favorites for the upcoming social season.

In the late 1880s, Mrs. Astor set up summer court in Newport, when she opened her Bellevue Avenue cottage, Beechwood. The cottage, bordered on three sides by a spacious piazza, had been a Newport attraction for many years. Mrs. Astor added a ballroom, the largest in Newport at that time. The elegant and tasteful Beechwood was quite different from the overpowering marble palaces that were built later by the Vanderbilts.

The dinner parties at Beechwood were the epitome of Gay Nineties elegance. Guests were immersed in an overwhelming atmosphere of gold, crystal, and flowers. Blue-liveried footmen (copied from Windsor Castle) served dinner on gold plates; roses and candelabra abounded. Guests would feast on ten courses over three or four hours.

For a time, a bitter battle raged over ownership of the title "Mrs. Astor." It seems the William Waldorf Astors set up housekeeping at the charming Beaulieu mansion, next to Mrs. Astor at Beechwood. William Waldorf, the son of John Jacob Astor III and Mrs. Astor's nephew, insisted that his wife, the former Mary Dahlgren Paul, be addressed as *The* Mrs. Astor. This caused some confusion at the Newport post office when letters for both women were addressed simply as "Mrs. Astor, Newport, Rhode Island." Eventually, with Ward McAllister's help, Caroline won the title on the basis of seniority and personality strength.

In any case, the Waldorf Astors soon moved to London, where they established the famous English branch of the family. The English Astors included the famous Lady Astor, the daughter-in-law of William Waldorf. Lady Astor, the former Nancy Langhorne, held a seat in the House of Commons for 25 years and was known as a flamboyant and witty campaigner. In one typical incident, while speaking in a farming district, she encountered a remark from a sarcastic farmer who said, "Say, missus, how many toes are there on a pig's foot?" She came back with the rejoinder, "Take off your boots man and count for yourself."

The American Astors were sometimes called the decadent Astors, while the English were known as the aristocratic Astors.

The marriage of Mrs. Astor's eldest daughter, Emily, to James Van Alen nearly resulted in a duel when her father insulted the Van Alens by insinuating that they were unworthy to marry Astors. William Astor later apologized.

Another daughter, Charlotte, married James Drayton of Philadelphia and later, had a lurid and widely reported love affair with Hallett Alsop

Borrowe, a vice-president of Equitable Life. In a gesture of hypocrisy, her playboy father disinherited her.

Ava Willing Astor before divorce

Mrs. Astor's son, John Jacob Astor IV, married Philadelphia socialite and outstanding beauty, Ava Willing. He was an army colonel and fought in the Spanish American War. In 1910, 46-year-old Colonel Jack Astor stunned society by divorcing Ava and marrying an 18-year-old girl, Madeleine Force. The newlyweds soon left for Europe, to wait until the incident blew over. When they returned in 1912, they sailed on the ill-fated cruise ship, *Titanic*. Astor went down with the ship, but his wife, pregnant with John Jacob Astor VI, was saved. Astor left an $87 million estate, $63 million of it in real estate.

In her later years, a disillusioned Mrs. Astor quietly withdrew from the front lines of society. She threw her last great ball in 1905, before going permanently into seclusion. Caroline Schermerhorn Astor, the queen of Newport, spent her last few years as a senile recluse in Beechwood mansion.

John Jacob Astor IV with wife Madeleine, 1911

KING LEHR

The Story of Harry and Bessie

The story of Harry and Bessie matches one of the most bizarre characters of the Gilded Age with a fabulously wealthy heiress caught in a web of unhappiness. To a large extent Elizabeth Drexel was a perfect fit for Harry Lehr's neurotically warped personality. She was naive, lonely, and above all, rigidly scrupulous.

Harry and Bessie on their wedding trip, 1901.

Harry Lehr, the son of a middle class Baltimore tobacco merchant, rose to become the court jester of Newport society. He was so entertaining at balls and got along so well with the matrons of society–none other than Alva, Tessie, Mamie and Mrs. Astor were his principal supporters–that he became entrenched as a social trendsetter. Although his meteoric career was initially self-made through intense and persistent honing of his skills as a doting *bon vivant*, it was Elizabeth (Bessie) who financed its continuation.

Harry initially established himself in Baltimore society as an agreeable and affable Gilded Age groupie. He gradually gathered attention as a party entertainer and was constantly in demand to play the piano, tell jokes, dance, speak French, or discourse on fashion or party planning.

His big break came when Mrs. Evelyn Townsend Burden invited him to Fairlawn, her Newport cottage. It was the beginning of Newport's lushest era, fertile ground for Harry's career development. Mrs. Astor soon recognized Harry's social skills, and with her sponsorship his career flourished rapidly.

Bessie,
at Court Ball,
Dresden

Under Mrs. Astor's tutelage, Harry's first Newport season was a great success. With his gift of showmanship and irresistible laugh, Harry became a prized decoration at dinner parties and balls. Harry was by no means a lazy layabout. As a professional sycophant and master student of high society, he ambitiously and eagerly honed his skills.

His first winter season in New York was triumphant as he dined regularly at Sherry's with Mrs. Astor and was intensely tracked by the society pages. Harry gradually evolved from a social participant to a leader and trendsetter.

Still virtually penniless, Harry managed to live the high life through his connections to the dowagers and matrons of New York society. His network of endorsements would be the envy of any modern-day professional athlete. The managements of Delmonico's and Sherry's were more than happy to have Harry dine *gratis*. He never paid at the Waldorf-Astoria, his imprimatur was enough. Jewelers loaned him their jewels, and tailors tailored for him at no charge. He was even on the payroll of a French champagne company.

When in Newport, he was an established guest, shuttling between mansions. Harry's repertoire included considerable gall and impudence.

This counterbalanced his fawning and doting. He developed this skill to such an extent that his insults became sought-after status symbols. When Mamie Fish and her husband were leaving a party early, he shot at them, "Sit down Fishes, you're not rich enough to leave first."

Always debonair and natty, Harry was blue-eyed and blond with an alto voice and a trademark laugh. The men of Newport society had little use for the likes of Harry Lehr, with his effete manner and love for women's fashions. They viewed him as the cause of more expenses as he helped their wives plan balls, try on gowns, and buy jewels.

Harry had no intention of relying on the munificence of Main Line society for long-term support. He needed a rich wife, but also one acceptable to society. Harry met Elizabeth Drexel Dahlgren through a mutual friend, Edith Gould. Elizabeth (Bessie), of the Main Line Philadelphia Drexels, was a recently widowed heiress, and in her autobiography *King Lehr and the Gilded Age*, she describes the meeting at Mrs. Gould's opera party: "Suddenly the lights went up and Edith Gould turned to me....

'My dear, I want you to meet the most amusing man in New York....'

I looked up into eyes of vivid blue that seemed to hold the very spirit of gaiety... He sat down at my side and we began to talk. In five minutes I had decided that Edith Gould was right; he was certainly the most amusing man that I had ever met. Conversation rippled around him. Impossible for anyone to be bored in his company."

Bessie was enamored of his charm and graciousness and rapidly fell in love. Harry had decided to marry Bessie but first invited her to lunch at Sherry's to meet the most powerful members of society at that time: Mrs. Astor, Tessie Oelrichs, Mamie Fish, and Alva Vanderbilt Belmont. Bessie must pass muster with this oligarchy, or Harry wouldn't consider marriage. Well, she did pass and describes the scene in her book. "As we rose to leave the restaurant I heard Mrs. Oelrichs say, 'I think she is delightful, Harry. We four are going to take her up. We will make her the fashion. You need have no fear...'"

On the way home Harry proposed.

Bessie intensely considered continuation of her "desperately lonely" life the way it was or starting a new life with Harry. She reflected on how her love for him was neither emotional nor passionate. She viewed it on a higher plane, one of respect, friendship, and affection. This perspective may have been the basis for her undoing.

She described their wedding ceremony with a sense of foreboding, and noted the absence of gaiety from Harry's vivid blue eyes; she only saw mockery.

On their wedding night, the future of the relationship was brought home to Bessie with stunning clarity. She planned a memorable evening at the Stafford Hotel in Baltimore.

"It was our wedding evening and I lingered over my dressing for this our first dinner alone, pinned a diamond brooch into my rose brocade gown, hoped that Harry would think me beautiful. In the adjoining dining room of our suite, the table was being laid–the sheaves of crimson roses I had ordered filled the room with their fragrance. Caviar, quails in aspic, his favorite brand of champagne, the cabinet of cigars I had bought for him; I had forgotten nothing. By the side of his plate lay the gold and enamel watch I had chosen so carefully. I wanted us both to remember this evening all our lives."

Soon the maid came in with a message that Harry was dining alone, and that she should do likewise. Later Harry appeared and told her the revolting truth.

He told Bessie that they would portray the happy couple in public, but in private he wanted nothing to do with her. He didn't love her, and he could never love her.

An overwhelmed Bessie could hardly whisper her response. "But why did you marry me?"

Harry, with his voice full of bitterness, told her the unvarnished truth: for her money, of course.

As Bessie was reeling with shock, Harry ended his sadistic speech by saying that they could get along quite well if she didn't come near him except in public, for in fact, she repulsed him.

On the surface, Harry and Bessie were the loving couple, but underneath the thin facade there was a black hole.

Throughout their marriage, Bessie was the unfortunate subject of Harry's constant ridicule and belittlement. Harry had no use for his wife, either as a companion or a mate; she was merely a tool to use to further his social career. Harry must have known that Bessie would endure her loveless fate, for she could not bring herself to divorce. Her staunch old-school Catholic mother would not brook divorce, and she feared hurting her deeply.

Even years later, when Bessie fell in love with a shadowy man whose identity was never disclosed, she would not give up Harry. She called this man Mister X in her autobiography. In sad irony, after her mother died and Bessie resolved to cast Harry away, she received the news that Mister X had died.

Harry loved women's things and gloried in their fashions, jewels, and parties. Although his sexual orientation was never clearly defined, he showed no romantic interest in the opposite sex.

Harry Lehr was the pivot of the festive set of society, and therefore, Bessie had to entertain lavishly, giving huge dinner parties. Harry aggressively pursued his vocation as social arbiter and mansion jester. He collaborated with the Great Triumverate to make and shape social policy. In their view, the stodgy and staid aristocracy of the early Gilded Age needed to be transformed into a more cosmopolitan, hedonistic, and iconoclastic ruling class.

In her book, Bessie describes Newport as a social Mecca. It was the pinnacle of social acceptance, and Harry Lehr was its self-proclaimed guru. He readily dispensed advice on how to enter Newport society. Bessie paints a vivid picture of exclusivity: "Every summer Harry Lehr and I went to Newport like everyone else in our world, for in those days so much prestige was attached to spending July and August at the most exclusive resort in America that to have neglected to do so would have exposed a definite gap in one's social armour." Anyone who had an established position in society went to Newport, there simply was no other way, "for Newport was the very Holy of Holies, the playground of the great ones of the earth from which all intruders were ruthlessly excluded by a set of cast-iron rules." Those who stayed away did so because they were afraid.

Harry Lehr stated it succinctly: "Avoid Newport like the plague until you are certain that you will be acceptable there. If you don't, it will be your Waterloo." Many a wealthy social climber tried to penetrate Newport outside the established system, only to flee in abject humiliation

Under Harry Lehr's tutelage, the morals of Newport society loosened. Many society women took weekday lovers while their husbands labored on Wall Street. The men often commuted to Newport on the Fall River steamships on Friday nights and spent most of their weekends at the Reading Room, or the Casino, or maybe retiring to their yacht in Newport harbor for a private party.

The parties and balls became much more lavish, and the conspicuous consumption led to disgust and cries of decadence from the general public. These excesses continued through the early part of the century, until the disruptions and fall-out from World War I put a serious crimp on lifestyles of such a grand scale.

Harry and Bessie traveled extensively in Europe and eventually bought a townhouse in Paris, and after World War I, they lived there most of the time. Harry eventually developed a brain disorder and died, mercifully bringing their twenty-eight year marriage to a close.

Bessie stayed in Paris, married an English lord and became a prominent social leader.

THE GREAT TRIUMVIRATE

Alva, Mamie and Tessie

The Great Triumvirate (Alva Belmont, Mamie Fish, and Tessie Oelrichs) consisted of three of the five most powerful women to rule Newport society throughout the Gilded Age, the other two being Mrs. Astor and Grace Wilson Vanderbilt.

A powerful trio–the driven Alva, the headstrong Tessie, and the abrasive Mamie collaborated to transform Newport society from the staid conservatism of Mrs. Astor to a more permissive and hedonistic institution. The three were unique in so many ways, but all possessed the unusual quality of spirited intelligence, a rare commodity among their peers.

Possibly the most influential and powerful woman of her time, **Alva Smith Vanderbilt Belmont** was the most durable member of the great Newport Triumvirate.

Alva dominated Newport society not through beauty or charm, but sheer willpower and boldness. Alva, an Alabama plantation belle, succeeded in marrying into two of the most powerful families of the Gilded Age. After gaining a sophisticated education at a French boarding school, she became a member of the southern aristocracy. In 1875, she visited the spa at White Sulfur Springs and met William K. Vanderbilt, the grandson of the famous Commodore. Then she accomplished what many post Civil War southern debutantes dreamed of: she married a Yankee millionaire.

It was Alva who succeeded in establishing the Vanderbilt name in the rarefied air at the social pinnacle. To do this, it was necessary to receive social recognition from Mrs. Caroline Astor, society's self-appointed Grand Dame. Initially, Mrs. Astor refused to acknowledge the social existence of the Vanderbilts, feeling threatened by their immense power and wealth. But Alva's gamesmanship was formidable. In 1883, Alva planned a spring ball at her Fifth Avenue mansion for the leading New York debutantes. Conveniently, Carrie Astor was just out of finishing school and ready to emerge into society. Carrie was crushed when no invitation was forthcoming; she was the only debutante excluded. Alva let it be known that since Mrs. Astor had never called at the Vanderbilt mansion, an invitation was impossible. Mrs. Astor finally capitulated and rode over to the Vanderbilt mansion. She stayed in her carriage as her footman delivered her calling card. That was all that was necessary, Carrie received her invitation, and

Alva

the Vanderbilts received the ultimate social recognition.

By the early 1890s, Alva firmly established hegemony in Newport. She collaborated with the preeminent architect of his time, Richard Morris Hunt, to build an eleven-million-dollar marble mansion. Marble House opened in 1892 and secured for Newport the leadership of the American Renaissance in classical architecture.

Alva was an imperious perfectionist and a heavy-handed tyrant. she never shied from educating her contemporaries on how to live and how to think. Even on a visit to Blair Castle in Scotland she criticized its authenticity.

In 1895, a battle royal erupted when daughter Consuelo balked at an arranged marriage to the Duke of Marlborough. Consuelo eventually relented and became one of several ill-fated American heiresses to marry a European title. In this fatally-flawed process, the American *nouveau riche* gained legitimacy for their status, and the European aristocrats gained immense financial power. Normally these were the only reasons. The usual result was a broken and bitter relationship, with the American woman getting short shrift in the form of abandonment, humiliation, and de facto robbery. This arrangement did little to help the United States balance of trade since more than $200 million of inherited capital was swept across the ocean.

A dowry of $10 million accompanied Consuelo to Blenheim Castle, the ducal residence of Charles Richard John Spencer-Churchill, the ninth Duke of Marborough. Entrance into the Churchill family was a costly venture, as millionaire Leonard Jerome could certainly have attested. Lord Randolph Churchill married his daughter Jennie (the mother of the great Winston) and significantly drained his sizable fortune in the process.

Both Consuelo and the Duke had hoped to marry their true loves. But these hopes were dashed in the face of duty and coercion.

Consuelo was not suited to the lifestyle of an English country duchess, and the daily tedium of her station gradually gave way to boredom. After eleven dismal years as mistress of the castle, she separated from the Duke, and they were eventually divorced.

At the same time Alva was negotiating with the hard-bargaining Churchills, her own marriage was unraveling rapidly. She and William K. were wholly incompatible. Her haughtiness contrasted considerably with his mild-mannered, relaxed, and unassuming demeanor. Devoted mostly to business and leisure, he rarely interfered in her management of the household.

After considerable domestic hostilities, including a series of intense and vituperative disputes aboard the Vanderbilt yacht on a cruise to India, they separated.

Even before the separation, William K. began spending more time on his yacht and with the Gilded Age equivalent of the international "Jet Set." He was rumored to be chasing women and neglecting the affairs of the New York Central Railroad, the flagship of the Vanderbilt empire.

In 1895, Alva shocked her contemporaries and became the first leading socialite to divorce her husband. Then in 1896, she stunned them again by marrying family friend Oliver Hazard Perry Belmont (reputed to be William K.'s best friend). Before the divorce Willie K. reportedly caught Perry Belmont in bed with Alva upstairs at Marble House.

From that point on, Alva was ostracized by the rest of the Vanderbilts, but not by the rest of society; she was too entrenched and ruthless for anyone to dare mount a successful coup. During the next summer in Newport, Alva resumed her dominant role as a member of the Great Triumverate. She closed Marble House and moved down the street (Bellevue Avenue) to govern Belcourt Castle.

Alva dominated Perry Belmont much as she had William K., but their marriage remained intact until Belmont died in 1908.

Later, she embraced the women's suffrage movement, casting her enormous influence and wealth into the effort. Alva decried the exploitation of her sex and eventually recanted the attitudes that forced her daughter into an unwanted marriage. As a result, Consuelo was granted an annulment.

After Belmont's death, Alva reopened Marble House, and in 1913, she held a large garden party and rally in support of the suffrage movement.

After the summer of 1916, Alva never reopened Marble House and left Newport for good. She spent her last years in France relentlessly promoting women's rights. She died in 1932.

Mrs. Herman Oelrichs possessed probably the most mundane heritage on Bellevue Avenue. Yet, she came to dominate Newport Society as a full-fledged member of the Great Triumvirate and mistress of the elegant mansion, Rosecliff.

Mrs. Oelrichs was the former Theresa Fair and was known as Tessie. Her childhood was nothing if not humble. Born in a California mining camp, Tessie was the daughter of James Fair, a lowly Irish immigrant who fled the devastating potato famine with his parents in 1843.

But for her father's extraordinary luck and tenacity, Tessie would likely have been just another frontier brat, shuttled from one squalid mining camp to another.

Tessie

Fair was a canny and calculating swashbuckler who came to the California goldfields by wagon train in 1849 and then proceeded to bide time building technical expertise in mining management. Fair focused his efforts not on placer mining (the washing of valuable minerals from sand deposits), but instead he searched for veins of gold-bearing quartz.

While working as a superintendent of a quartz mill in Angels Camp, California, he met Theresa Rooney, a pretty and winsome young widow. They married and had four children: Tessie, Virginia (known as Birdie), Charles and James.

Around 1860, Fair made his move and joined the rush to the Nevada silver mines. Several years later in Virginia City, he formed a partnership with three other astute Irishmen, and they bought large tracts of mining claims.

Up to this time, San Francisco bankers controlled Nevada mining development, but Fair and his associates bought up their holdings and transferred them to the group's newly-organized Bank of Nevada. They began vigorously digging shafts and tunnels, and in their Consolidated Virginia Mine they stumbled upon a pocket of gold and silver that may have been the most valuable single ore pocket ever found. It was Fair's dogged pursuit of a meager, meandering vein that led to the discovery of this astonishing bonanza.

The yield from the Consolidated Virginia Mine was so vast that it shook the market for gold and silver. The four partners went on to control the silver mining industry, and their take from the Comstock Lode amounted to more than $100 million. Fair parlayed his share into real estate, railroads, and other enterprises, and his eventual wealth was estimated at around $50 million.

Immense power and wealth unleashed the dark side of James Fair, and he became an accomplished practitioner of avarice, corruption, and blatant debauchery. He cheated in business, ran a successful but corrupt campaign for the U. S. Senate, and was an extensive womanizer. He had little use for the Senate and rarely participated in its functions.

Claiming adultery, his wife sued for divorce in 1883. The divorce settlement granted Mrs. Fair one third of the estate and custody of Tessie and Birdie. Fair was charged with the care of Charles and James.

Theresa took Tessie and Birdie away to a life of refinement and private tutors. It seems the female Fairs were cut from a different bolt than the males. Fair had little interest in fatherhood and exercised limited control over the boys.

Son James nearly drank himself to death and eventually committed suicide. Charles was also a heavy drinker. He married against his father's will and was nearly disinherited. In 1902, Charles and his wife were killed in a high-speed auto accident near Paris.

The sisters decided to pursue a more discreet and genteel lifestyle, one of social position and brokered marriages. But Tessie was determined to broker her own marriage, and after sifting through a crop of fortune hunters, layabouts, and no-accounts, she settled on Herman Oelrichs, the son of a wealthy German shipping magnate. The Oelrichs family owned the North German Lloyd line of transatlantic ocean liners.

The spectacular San Francisco wedding (in 1890) was a magnificent social display attended by a large number of aristocrats and luminaries of the day. James Fair was not invited.

Herman's amiable personality contrasted sharply with the feisty and headstrong Tessie. Although he was ten years her senior, the marriage made great social sense.

Tessie's mother died in 1891 (the same year the sisters purchased Rosecliff), and James fair died in 1894 after living his last years alone in the Lick House, San Francisco. As a result, the sisters' net worth increased substantially. However, Fair left several wills, and his lecherous lifestyle produced a host of claimants to his fortune. For seven years, an incessant series of court battles depleted the estate and consumed much of Tessie's attention before all matters were finally settled.

After the wedding, Tessie's social sights were set on New York and Newport, and although Herman loved San Francisco, he deferred to her desires, and they moved East.

If Tessie's marriage was a sensible social alliance, then Birdie's was a brilliant social coup. In 1899, Tessie negotiated a match between her younger sister and William K. Vanderbilt II, the son of Alva and William K. Vanderbilt and great grandson of the famous Commodore.

Birdie may have been Tessie's alter ego. Tiny and mild-mannered, she contrasted sharply with the headstrong and regal Tessie. An 1894 picture at Bailey's Beach shows Birdie soaking wet and decked in a neck-to-ankle black "bathing suit" dress, with a big hat extending over her slightly pug nose. She cut a comical sight by today's standards, but she was right on the mark for the Gilded Age.

The society pages reported Birdie's wedding extensively. Just like Tessie's wedding, all the minutia was covered. The elite of New York society attended the reception at the Oelrich's Fifth-Avenue mansion. Vanderbilt gave his new wife a $75,000 pearl necklace.

They were light years from the dusty streets of Angel's Camp.

With time, Tessie and Herman gradually drifted apart. The romantic mismatch so common to socially-contracted marriages became apparent, and they began to live as far apart as they felt. He lived casually in his beloved San Francisco mansion, while she lorded over Rosecliff.

Tessie compensated for this marital vacuum by a single-minded devotion to her role as a baron of Newport society. She pretended intimacy with her husband and never publicly acknowledged the rift. Despite their geographic separation of continental proportions, she maintained the facade.

Tessie also feigned satisfaction with her powerful career on the Great Triumvirate. Blanche Oelrichs (Tessie's niece), in her autobiography, describes her aunt as seemingly restless, unhappy, and unfulfilled.

Tessie had the energy of a dervish and was completely immersed in her role. She ruled Rosecliff with drill instructor mentality, the mansion had to be spit-shined every day, and woe to the servant who was not equal to her standards. Her wrathful tongue scourged many an ear.

She masked her melancholy effectively as she dashed around Newport in her electric auto or whisked into the Casino flashing her classic Irish beauty and regal grace in huge hats with lace dresses adorning her hourglass figure.

No doubt, like many like many intelligent and capable women of the time, she felt unfulfilled in her role and stifled in a society with norms so restrictive on female behavior and vocations. She turned to social and domestic pursuits as outlets for her boundless energy and found they came up short. They simply weren't enough. However, Tessie had the added advantages bestowed by immense wealth and was therefore able to stamp an indelible imprint on history.

After Herman survived the 1906 San Francisco earthquake, Tessie was so overwhelmed with relief that she vowed to repair their relationship. These efforts were dashed, however, when Herman returned to New York but visited his Fifth-Avenue club before seeing his repentant wife. Tessie, after redecorating his room, buying him a new wardrobe, and laying out romantic supper, was enraged and resumed the status quo.

Tessie and Herman never reconciled, and he died of a heart attack aboard a North German Lloyd liner. But there was one final bitter pill for Tessie.

Herman had left his meager half-million dollar estate to his relatively unprosperous brother Charles. He wrongly assumed that Tessie would be satisfied with her millions. She contested the will and won half the estate.

Like so many others of her genre, Tessie spent her final days in a senile fantasy land, reliving old dinner parties and replaying the social highlights of day's past.

Mrs. Stuyvesant (Mamie) Fish, the third member of the Great Triumvirate, was surely the most colorful of Newport hostesses. Mamie was a master satirist and an iconoclast with a great sense of humor. She had little use for the trappings of her class. She always seemed bored by her milieu, and yet, she threw the most innovative and enjoyable parties. She insulted nearly everyone and was a gifted purveyor of one-liners.

Mamie hailed from Crossways, a magnificent Ocean Drive mansion with a commanding view of the pounding sea. Crossways has an overscaled Colonial portico supported by four Corinthian columns, but, consistent with the Fishes' relatively modest net worth, it doesn't exhibit the spectacle or monumentality of its exotic Bellevue Avenue cousins. Mamie would insist, "We're not rich, we have only a few million."

Mamie (born Mary Ann) had only a rudimentary education and could barely read or write. She was far from beautiful, save her sharp deep-black eyes. But she was the most sought after hostess in Newport.

Even though she was hardly educated, Mamie still seemed better suited to a more rewarding and meaningful life than that of a Gilded Age hostess.

Mamie married Stuyvesant Fish, her childhood sweetheart and possibly the most tolerant baron Newport has ever seen. Unlike many others, their marriage endured because they truly loved and understood each other. Stuyvesant was a professional manager and became president of the Illinois Central Railroad in 1887. Mr. Fish had no interest in society or ostentation, but when dealing with his wife, he was a paradigm of patience, with his unruffled manner and unpretentious attitude.

Mamie

Mamie's tumultuous public life belied an extremely happy private life; in sharp contrast to her peers, she was a devoted wife and mother.

She was determined to attain social prominence by following an unorthodox path, and when she teamed up with the convoluted Harry Lehr (which she often did), the results were unpredictable. To Mamie, boredom was the ultimate sin.

Mamie worshipped no sacred cows; she refused to participate in the social whirl of teas, card-calling, and ritualistic drives along Bellevue Avenue; she detested operas and musicales and would usually chatter endlessly throughout the program, much to the chagrin of the other guests. She got into a big row with James Van Alen when, knowing her incorrigible behavior, he invited only Mr. Fish and Mrs. Lehr (excluding Mamie and Harry Lehr) to a musicale. After she confronted Van Alen at Bailey's Beach and threatened to sabotage the affair, he relented but insisted that Mamie and Harry be exiled to the terrace while the music played.

Mamie had this disarming way of calling everyone "Sweet pet" or "Lamb," mainly because she was notorious for remembering names, but it also suited her mountainous indifference. She would always welcome guests to her balls with an impatient "Howdy do, howdy do," moving them along with obvious annoyance. Her sharp tongue could cut ice, and her barbs were thrown with deadly accuracy.

She once gave a luncheon for 50 ladies and refused to attend. She sat upstairs at Crossways and wouldn't come down despite the entreaties of her maid. "But Mrs. Fish, you invited them two weeks ago," the maid pleaded. Mamie dismissed her with a wave, "Tell them I've changed my mind."

Her one-liners were classic. "Make yourselves at home," she would tell her guests. "And believe me, there is no one who wishes you were there more than I do."

Once while her orchestra was playing "Home, Sweet Home," a male friend begged Mamie for one more two-step. She replied, "There are just two steps more for you, one upstairs to get your coat and the other out to your carriage."

Even Harry Lehr, who had married the wealthy Elizabeth Drexel Dahlgren, was not safe. When he asserted that Mamie's favorite flower must be the climbing rose, she retorted, "And I know yours, pet. The Marigold." Mamie even told Alva Belmont she looked like a toad.

The balls and dinners at Crossways were renowned; the minuscule staff (15 servants) and modest budget managed to produce Newport's most entertaining affairs.

Mamie's quest was to dominate and enliven society, and in the process she set new standards for entertaining. Breaking the mold of staid cotillions, she opened Crossways to all manner of lively entertainment. Dinner guests were treated to fetes ranging from a Marie Dresser comedy skit, to the chorus line from The Merry Widow, to an exhibition of John L. Sullivan's muscles. She even allowed celebrities to dine in the rarefied company of society's elite–a radical practice at the time.

Eschewing the lumbering three-hour dinners of other hostesses, Mamie regularly served eight courses in less than an hour (her record was 30 minutes). Then it was on to the special entertainment.

Harry Lehr was Mamie's confidant and collaborator. On several occasions, they teamed up to surprise and amuse Newport society. They created the hilarious "Monkey Dinner" and the bizarre "Dogs' Dinner." They even fooled all of Newport society when Harry Lehr impersonated the Czar of Russia.

On this occasion, Mamie had planned to invite Grand Duke Boris of Russia, a house guest at Mrs. Ogden Goelet's Ochre Court, but her plans were scuttled when the two women feuded. To avoid a major embarrassment (her invitations were already sent), Harry Lehr appeared at Crossways disguised in medals and robes and entered with a flourish amidst bows and curtsies. Speaking in broken English, he reviewed an astounded but laughing line of guests.

No one was immune to her abrasive tongue. It even led to the sacking of her husband after nearly 20 years as president of the Illinois Central, when E. H. Harriman, a formidable railroad baron, revengefully orchestrated a coup against

Crossways

Fish at an Illinois Central board meeting. The meeting erupted into a heated argument and ended with the decking of a board member by the fist of an enraged Stuyvesant Fish. Mr. Fish was out of a job and blackballed from the railroads.

The cause? Mamie again.

Mamie found Harriman's wife, Mary, unacceptable for social recognition (too dull), so she snubbed her from a Crossways' tea party. After Harriman learned of this and of other insults at the party, he swore revenge, and Stuyvesant was his target.

Even though she invited them to fabulous and meticulously planned parties, Mamie seemed to repudiate her guests and always viewed them as a burden. It was the paradox of Mamie Fish: she recognized the triviality and senselessness of Gilded Age society, yet she aggressively sought its limelight.

To the end, Mamie was undaunted, relentless, and unswerving, and she still maintained her dominant social position in spite of her splendidly arrogant attitude–maybe because of it.

Mamie died of a stroke in 1915, just before her annual June 8 birthday party.

THE VANDERBILTS

Newport's First Family

The Vanderbilts are certainly the Gilded Age family most closely associated with Newport. Family members were intimately intertwined in Newport life. They owned two of the most prestigious mansions (the Breakers and Marble House), several lesser "cottages," and two large farms (Oakland and Sandy Point). Their matrons (Alva Vanderbilt Belmont, Alice Gwynne Vanderbilt, and Grace Wilson Vanderbilt) dominated Newport society, and their men were heavily involved in social clubs, charities, and leisure activities.

Cornelius Vanderbilt, Senior (1794-1877) established the family fortune, and when he died in 1877, he was the richest man in America. The legendary Cornelius, Senior (known as the Commodore) was uncouth, shrewd, and driven. He was a visionary and an empire builder. The Commodore parlayed a humble Staten Island pole-powered ferryboat into a steamboat conglomerate transporting passengers and freight all along the Atlantic and Pacific coasts.

The trail-blazing Commodore established a lucrative New York-to-San Francisco transportation service. This innovative route traversed Nicaragua in an adventure-packed journey through river rapids and mountain jungles. The Commodore had found a way to shorten the trip to California and drew lucrative gold-rush traffic away from competitors who still used the isthmus of Panama. He even developed plans to build the first Central American canal, but they met stiff political opposition and never came to fruition.

However, shipping was only the beginning as the Commodore vastly expanded his fortune and power through railroads. Vanderbilt began buying railroads in the early 1860s when their economic importance was increasing rapidly. The Commodore built railroads, acquired railroads, consolidated railroads, and bribed legislators for rights of way and special preferences related to railroads. He established the New York Central, with its routes to the Great Lakes and vital link to the West, as the flagship of the Vanderbilt empire.

The Commodore was big and strong. His curly hair and bushy sideburns framed a handsome face etched with distinction. He loved good cigars, but drank little alcohol, considering the practice a waste of time. He had scant education and a large storehouse of profanities which he used profusely.

Throughout his life, Vanderbilt attracted many enemies who were as ruthless as he, but few were as shrewd or as brassy. In confrontations, the Commodore usually came out on top and sometimes in spectacular fashion.

On several occasions he bested his archenemy, an unscrupulous manipulator named Daniel Drew. But one particular confrontation proved enormously beneficial to the Commodore.

No altar boy himself, the Commodore had paid off an extremely corrupt New York legislature to approve consolidation of two of his railroads, the Hudson River and the Harlem. This move would reduce operating expenses and greatly benefit Vanderbilt.

However, Daniel Drew persuaded the New York legislators to double cross Vanderbilt into believing he would get his way. The conspirators knew the price of Harlem stock would rise sharply on wind of the consolidation, so they planned to sell the stock short at the high price. Since a short sale is a promise to deliver a stock at the agreed price at some future date, they planned to buy the stock later at a much depressed price (after they voted against Vanderbilt's bill) and cover their short sales. In this way, they could buy low having already sold very high.

As expected the price rose to 150, and Drew and the legislators sold short.

Then the legislators voted against the consolidation and watched the stock price quickly plunge to 90. The legislators and Drew waited to buy at an even lower price, but the Commodore, his back against the wall, began a buying binge of Harlem stock. He mortgaged and sold properties in a desperate attempt to raise cash. Soon he and his brokers had bought all the shares, and there were none available for the short sellers to buy in order to make good on their promise. Vanderbilt controlled them all!

The conspirators would have to buy from him; there was no other source. A triumphant Vanderbilt set his price at $285 per share. Vanderbilt made $25 million, and after several corrupt legislators were thrown into personal bankruptcy, he had the great, albeit ironic, satisfaction of breaking up a most dishonest legislative body.

Vanderbilt's business philosophy was control and growth. He believed money was a means and not an end. To the Commodore, the goal was power and achievement. Unfortunately for the family fortune, Cornelius, Senior didn't take the time to train his son and principal heir, William Henry in these values.

William Henry Vanderbilt (1821-1885) increased the family fortune and became the richest man in the world. But although only one generation removed from the self-made Commodore, William Henry lacked the drive, the edge, the hunger necessary for empire building. He was more materialistic and concerned with protecting the fortune rather than expanding the empire.

Like his father, William Henry was a large man with strong features. His reddish sideburns were so outrageously overgrown that they fell over his collar and along his shoulders. William Henry had a passion for trotting horses, and in 1883 at New York's Fleetwood Park, he drove his famous pair of Aldine and Maud S. to a world record for the mile.

Vanderbilt's other avocation was collecting art. He traveled extensively in Europe in search of landscape and animal pictures. He didn't like Impressionism, which was so popular at the time, and he wouldn't even look at nude paintings. He jammed his Fifth Avenue mansion with paintings to such an untasteful extent that the result was a hodgepodge.

In an attempt to diversify family wealth, William Henry sold large blocks of stock in Vanderbilt railroads. He invested in safe government securities and railroad bonds. When he retired in 1883, his interest and dividend income amounted to more than $10 million per year. And when he died in 1885, he held $73 million in government bonds, plus $22 million in railroad bonds and $2 million in mortgages and other paper.

His entire estate was nearly $200 million, and most of it was bequeathed to his two oldest sons Cornelius Vanderbilt II ($67 million) and William Kissam Vanderbilt ($65 million). Lesser sums of $10 million were given to each of William Henry's four daughters and two other sons Frederick William and George Washington II.

Even though the family still controlled most of the Commodore's railroad empire, control had been split and therefore diluted. Although Cornelius II and William Kissam (known as Willlie K.) assumed the chairmanships of the major railroads in the Vanderbilt system, management of the railroads was ceasing to be family business. Bankers like J. Pierpont Morgan and professional managers played an increasingly important role in the operations. Also, the two young railroad barons were not as intense or single-minded about the business as William Henry or the Commodore.

The two brothers had little in common, Cornelius II spent a great deal of time on charities and church activities, while Willie K. developed the lifestyle of a Gilded Age jet-setter, indulging in the leisure time activities of the born-rich.

After William Henry's death, the fabric of the Vanderbilt family began to gradually unravel. With the wealth dispersed and control of the railroads diluted, Vanderbilt interest and attention focused on a variety of diversions, and rifts and animosities erupted between family members.

The three principal schisms centered on that old nemesis: marriage and divorce in contravention to family wishes. The most controversial was the marriage of Cornelius III to Grace Wilson. Lesser controversies revolved around Frederick's marriage to Louise Torrance and Alva Smith's divorce of Willie K. and her subsequent remarriage to Perry Belmont.

The Commodore's heirs failed to create a dynasty like the Rockefellers, the Du Ponts, or the Fords. They lost control of the railroad empire and lacked the drive to regain or rebuild it. They became aimless gentlemen spenders or financiers. Most viewed wealth as privilege and not something for constructive use. But blame must be shared collectively. The Commodore didn't take the time to pass his philosophy on to his son William Henry. William Henry in turn attempted to conserve capital and didn't understand the importance of building, and he never instilled in Cornelius II or Willie K. the value of combining wealth with high purpose and personal abilities.

Also, the key Vanderbilt heirs (Cornelius II, Willie K., Frederick William, George Washington II, Cornelius III, Willie K. II, Alfred Gwynne, Reggie and Harold) lacked the direction and the desire to build a dynasty, even though some accomplished much.

Cornelius Vanderbilt II (1843-1899) was the oldest son of William Henry and grandson of the Commodore. The Commodore intended for his grandson and namesake to eventually take over as head of the family and the railroad empire. He made certain that Cornelius II worked in the railroads and took a personal interest in his career.

The Commodore would probably not have wanted the empire split as it was in William Henry's will. But as William Henry diversified family wealth by selling railroad stocks in favor of other investments, he also diversified family control by splitting power between his sons.

Cornelius II's lifestyle would probably not have pleased the Commodore either. The old man would have no use for Cornelius' penchant for charitable and religious activities. He donated much of his income and time to this effort; he was a Sunday school teacher and vestryman at his church.

Cornelius was a workaholic, and he diligently tackled his job with the railroads. When William Henry retired, Cornelius and Willie K. took over the chairmanships of the principal railways, with Cornelius getting the

Cornelius Vanderbilt II (1843-1899)

New York Central and the Michigan Central. So when William Henry died two years later, the brothers were firmly entrenched in the business.

Although Cornelius (and Willie K. to a lesser degree) was conscientious about family (meaning railroad) responsibilities, he lacked the intensity and vision necessary to build and preserve the empire. He depended heavily on banker J.P. Morgan and others for advice even though their interests did not always coincide with the Vanderbilts.

Cornelius II was heavily involved in Newport life, principally as a pillar of the community. Yet ironically he is best known for creating The Breakers, a mansion that clashed so much with his phlegmatic personality.

A stern, solemn, seemingly ascetic man (didn't smoke or drink), Cornelius wasn't given to frivolity. He shunned society in favor of Sunday school. For Cornelius, the Breakers was the ultimate paradox. It was by far the most lavish and ostentatious private residence in Newport, if not the world. The only reasonable explanation for this incongruity lies with **Alice Claypoole Gwynne**, Cornelius' wife.

By the late 1880s, Alice Vanderbilt entered into a bitter rivalry with Alva Vanderbilt (Willie K.'s wife) for social dominance of the Vanderbilt family. The indomitable Alva had Alice outgunned when it came to manipulation and maneuvering, but as the wife of the head of the Vanderbilt family, Alice was not about to capitulate. And her ace in the hole was The Breakers

In 1892, Cornelius Vanderbilt II selected the prolific and prominent architect, Richard Morris Hunt to design a stunning mansion on Newport's Ochre Point at the edge of the cliffs. Ironically, Hunt had designed Marble House for Willie K. and Alva. But The Breakers was his greatest achievement.

The Grand Staircase at the Breakers

Certainly Hunt must have consulted extensively with Alice, since The Breakers, with its breathtaking opulence, was so out of character for Cornelius. Hunt chose the style of European Renaissance, and modeled The Breakers after a Northern Italian villa. This imposing palace stands on the edge of the Atlantic Ocean overlooking the pounding surf.

Amazingly, Hunt took only two years to build The Breakers. The project was a tremendous undertaking, and included a workforce of hundreds of laborers and craftsmen, many imported from Europe. The logistics involved the selection and transportation of materials from Europe and Africa as well as coordination and collaboration with several noted architects and artists.

In France, craftsmen assembled (down to the last detail) the Grand Salon, which was then disassembled, crated and shipped to Newport. Then to ensure perfection, the same French craftsmen traveled to Newport and reassembled the room in The Breakers.

In construction Hunt used steel beams, stone, brick, and tile. But fearing fire (the old wooden Breakers had recently burned to the ground), he used no wood. With fire still in mind, Hunt segregated the furnace several hundred feet from the house and connected it with a massive tunnel.

For the interior he imported marble, alabaster and stone from Italy,

France, and Africa. The entrance is guarded by enormous, but perfectly balanced oak doors. Weighing many tons, they still move at the slight push of a finger. Behind the oak doors, between the vestibule and the entrance hall, are a pair of huge hand-wrought, iron-grilled doors paneled with plate glass and weighing over seventy tons.

The Great Hall in the center of the mansion is awesome. It rises forty-five feet, and its majestic magnificence is numbing. The Great Hall rises through two full floors to a ceiling painted to look like a blue, cloud-dotted sky. Carvings and marble plaques adorn the walls faced with French Caen stone. Huge fluted pilasters decorate the perimeter, and carved acorns and oak leaves (the Vanderbilt symbol) abound. The rooms on the second floor open onto balconies overlooking the Great Hall.

A grand circular staircase, with fountain beneath, divides at a landing and rises gracefully to a balcony. A huge (twenty-four by eighteen feet) Flemish tapestry overlooks the landing.

The billiard room, made of pale-green Cippolino marble from floor to ceiling, is trimmed in mahogany and contains an English weighing chair that gives the weight of the sitter in stones.

The most lavish and ornate is probably the dining room. A ceiling painting of Aurora at Dawn overlooks this spacious two-story room, which is surrounded by twelve massive red Numidian marble columns. Two huge chandeliers hang from a ceiling containing life-size figures set into arches.

The outside of this 17th century stone palace exhibits double loggias (open galleries) with different sized arches, ornamental marble columns and a variety of towers and terraces. The renowned Olmstead firm of land-scape architects designed the grounds.

The house has seventy rooms, with thirty-three for the servants on a hidden fourth floor. The breathtaking opulency and sumptuous ornamenta-tion is saturating to the senses, and it is difficult to imagine anyone living comfortably in this overwhelming atmosphere.

But this was the home of Alice of the Breakers, and she clearly had the title of the biggest and best. In his memoirs, her grandson, Cornelius Vanderbilt IV describes the Breakers and his grandmother:

"Downstairs, the kitchen was the size of a small house, with five im-mense wood-burning ranges, each with eight or ten burners. The butler's pantry was two decks high, and lined to the ceiling with fine glassware and china, all chosen from samples brought to Mrs. Vanderbilt's house, for it was said she had never entered a shop. At The Breakers she could give a dinner party for two hundred, it was rumored, without calling in extra

help. And each morning, Mrs. Vanderbilt, wearing immaculate white gloves, inspected her household, running a gloved finger over table tops and picture frames and stair railings. And when she was through, the gloves had better be white!"

The Breakers Grand Salon, c. 1900

Cornelius Vanderbilt II died in 1899 at age fifty-six. Many said he worked himself to death with worry and intensity over the railroads, numerous charities and family responsibilities. Most people were unaware of the extent of his charitable involvement (he was a director of several large charities). Messages of condolence flowed in steadily for months.

Cornelius was a kind man, beloved by nearly everyone, but ironically he seemed unhappy and incapable of enjoying his vast wealth. And despite all his kindness, he sadly refused to reconcile with his eldest son, Cornelius Vanderbilt III (Neily), who had irrevocably angered his father by marrying the "wrong woman."

Even though Cornelius II spent and gave away vast amounts of his fortune, he still managed to increase his initial inheritance. His estate amounted to almost $73 million. Alfred Vanderbilt (second son) received the bulk of the estate (almost $43 million). Neily, his eldest, was virtually cut out; his share was $1,500,000.

Alice of the Breakers inherited a $7 million trust fund, and of course she got The Breakers. The other four children shared the rest of the estate.

Cornelius II clearly wanted Neily disowned, for the will specified that if Alfred died, the estate would go to brother Reggie, and if he died, it would be shared by the girls. However, after Neily threatened litigation, Alfred granted him an additional $6 million.

After her husband's death, Alice of The Breakers settled into the role of family matriarch. She never fully mended the rift with Neily or his wife, the strong-willed Grace Wilson Vanderbilt. But occasionally Alice attended balls at their Newport mansion, Beaulieu.

Alice had a long reign at The Breakers, and became an institution in Newport's social scene. She died in 1934 at age 89. The Breakers is now owned by the Preservation Society of Newport County and is open for public viewing.

Alice of the Breakers with daughter Gladys, 1907

Frederick William Vanderbilt (1856-1938) was the third son of William Henry Vanderbilt. Frederick, after graduating from Yale, spent most of his time immersed in the operation of the Vanderbilt railroads, and he was more prepared for the business than any of his brothers.

However, when William Henry died he left Frederick only $10 million and no real control over the Vanderbilt railways. Frederick angered his father when he married (in 1878) against his wishes. Louise Torrance was twelve years older than Frederick and divorced from his first cousin. But the headstrong and handsome Frederick (he had a handlebar mustache and slicked-down hair parted in the middle) married her anyway. Louise Torrance came from a reputable but only moderately well-off family. She was known as one of the great (but pampered) beauties of New York, and she longed for the grand lifestyle. William Henry was furious, but this fury boiled beneath the surface and was only completely apparent after the will was disclosed.

Having been shut out of the Vanderbilt super fortune, Frederick turned to banking and investments. In this arena he was a financial genius, and he multiplied his $10 million into an estate worth $76 million.

Frederick was not a big spender, and compared to other Vanderbilts, his tastes were simple. However, he had several houses and yachts, and he often kept a million dollars in his checking account. His mansion at Hyde Park, New York is now a national historic site run by the federal government. He also had mansions in Newport, Florida and Bar Harbor, Maine, and a Japanese fishing camp in the Adirondack Mountains.

Like so many other Barons of the Gilded Age, Frederick was a reserved introvert and not caught up in the social whirl that so captivated his wife. During parties he would often slip out the side door of the mansion to wander the grounds for hours.

In 1890, Frederick began building Rough Point, his massive stone mansion at Newport, and Louise entered a career of lavish entertainment. Rough Point sits near the bottom of Bellevue Avenue, atop the rocky cliffs overlooking the ocean.

However, Newport life bored Frederick, and by 1895 he began work on his Hyde Park estate. Later he divided his time between Newport, New York, and cruising on his various yachts.

In his will, Frederick (he had no children) divided his fortune between several charities and his wife's relatives (with a large share left to Louise's niece, Mrs. James Van Alen). In the will, his festering animosity toward the family for being denied control of the railroads surfaced. No Vanderbilt was left a penny.

George Washington Vanderbilt II (1862-1914), the youngest son of William Henry, showed little interest in railroads or high society. George used his $10 million inheritance to establish an enormous barony in the North Carolina mountains.

He bought about 125,000 acres and hired the eminent architect, Richard Morris Hunt to design the Biltmore, a huge French Renaissance chateau. The ostentatious mansion, built in 1895, has 250 rooms (including 40 bedrooms), a 75-foot-high medieval banquet hall, and library space for 25,000 volumes. He employed the master landscape architect Frederick Law Olmstead (who designed Central Park and worked on several Newport mansions) to lay out the grounds. The Biltmore was a self-sufficient fiefdom with 750 employees working on farms, forestry projects, or in the estate's private village. Nearly the entire Vanderbilt clan traveled in private railroad cars to spend the Christmas of 1895 at the Biltmore.

After a few years as a country baron, George tired of the Biltmore estate and went tiger hunting in India. George was an eccentric intellectual who repudiated high society and business. He would much rather study ancient Greek and did, translating several contemporary works into that classic language. When he died in 1914, George was a poor Vanderbilt, and other than real estate and a $5 million trust fund, he had only $900,000.

William Kissam Vanderbilt (1849-1920), after inheriting an enormous sum, settled down to a life of serious leisure. In 1886, he built the fabulous yacht, *Alva*. At 285 feet she was the largest and most expensive ($500,000) private ship in the world. The three cabins on the main deck were steel plated and paneled with teak on the outside and mahogany on the inside. Willie K.'s personal quarters consisted of nine rooms. The dining room was 32 feet by 18 feet with nine-foot ceilings, a fireplace, a piano, a skylight, and two brass chandeliers. The 16 feet by 18 feet library was paneled in French walnut and had its own fireplace and skylight. The *Alva* carried a crew of fifty-three including a doctor.

In 1887, Willie K. took his wife Alva and their children on extensive cruises to the Caribbean, Europe, and the Middle East. Willie K. brought several friends including the handsome and charming bachelor, O.H.P. Belmont.

Perry Belmont spent much time alone with Alva while Willie K. was off on his frequent and inexplicable side trips. This was an obvious precursor to eventual problems, since a few years later Alva shocked society by divorcing Willie K. and marrying Perry Belmont.

By the late 1880s, Willie K. was spending increasingly less time on New York Central Railroad business. Instead, his attention was on social diversions and playing the role of amiable clubman.

Along with the other leaders of New York society, Willie K. and Alva began spending their summers in Newport. Some of the Commodore's daughters had been regular summer visitors to the city, but they had not dominated its social life as later Vanderbilt matrons would. Even old William Henry was remembered for driving his trotters around Newport's streets.

Alva was determined to play a leading role in high society, and Willie K. promoted this effort in 1888, when he commissioned Richard Morris Hunt to build a marble palace near the cliffs on Newport's Bellevue Avenue.

Marble House opened in 1892 and secured for Newport the leadership of the American Renaissance in classical architecture. Patterned after the Trianon at Versailles, this most sumptuous residence (which still stands and is now a museum) has an imposing two-story entrance portico supported by gigantic fluted Corinthian columns. The ornate entrance grille weighs over ten tons. The entrance hall rises over twenty feet and is lined with yellow Italian marble. Throughout the house the ornamentation is abundant with scenes and figures from Greek and Roman mythology. The rooms contain a variety of styles. The elegant dining room is faced with dark Numidian marble from Africa. And the Gothic Room and the rococo-style library contrast sharply with the Gold Room which is a stunning display of gilt.

In 1893, the William K. Vanderbilts took another ocean voyage aboard Willie K.'s new yacht, the *Valiant* (the *Alva* had sunk after a collision near Martha's Vineyard). With seventeen-year-old daughter Consuelo and Perry Belmont among the guests, they departed for India on what was to be their longest and last cruise together.

In her memoirs, Consuelo Vanderbilt recalls the dreadful cruise as a series of "continual disagreements" and shouting matches between her parents. The cruise ended in a final blowout at Bombay, India. Willie K. and Alva hastily left the yacht and headed to Paris. Soon Alva took the children to England and then back to Newport in the fall of 1894. Willie K. stayed in Paris, and rumors described liaisons with a beautiful Parisian lady. He already had an established reputation for philandering. When he returned to New York, he stayed at the Metropolitan Club, and visited Newport only for a few days to pick up his personal effects from Marble House.

Alva quickly filed for divorce, and in March of 1895, she became the first prominent American socialite to divorce her husband.

After the divorce, Alva waged a successful war against the Vanderbilt family and other socialites who attempted to ostracize her from Society. In the face of severe slurs on her reputation, anyone with a weaker personality than the indomitable Alva could not have maintained her position in Society. But her position in the Great Triumverate was ironclad, and any matron who valued her social future wisely attended Alva's first ball that following summer at Marble House.

Although the Vanderbilt family refused to even acknowledge her existence, their efforts were futile as Alva counterattacked, claiming she was the first society woman with nerve enough to divorce her husband (although many others would like to), and she threatened to blackball anyone siding with the Vanderbilts.

Alva was awarded Marble House in the divorce settlement, and in the summer of 1895 she held a fabulous ball for five hundred guests. The guest of honor was the young ninth Duke of Marlborough, Alva's hand-picked choice for daughter Consuelo's husband. Alva and Consuelo received guests amidst the luxurious dark pink Numidian marble of the dining room.

It was an extravagant floral fete featuring elaborate decorations of water hyacinths, lotus flowers, and swarms of live hummingbirds, butterflies, and bees. Nine French chefs prepared a sumptuous feast, with one course consisting of 400 mixed birds. The favors were Louis XIV-style fans, watch cases, and mirrors–all hand-made in Paris and each bearing the Marble House medallion. The oriental silk lanterns that hung all over the grounds were hand-made in China.

After intense negotiations, Consuelo and the Duke were betrothed. It was a significant social coup for Alva, but it cost Willie K. plenty. The frail and fragile Consuelo would become the ninth Duchess of Marlborough, princess of the Holy Roman Empire and mistress of Blenheim Castle, but the Duke would get $2,500,000 in railroad stock plus an annual allowance of $100,000.

The wedding was a spectacular ceremony at St. Thomas Episcopal Church in New York. The interior of the huge church was festooned with flowers top to bottom, and a sixty-piece orchestra played classical music. It was Alva's moment of glory; she had brought the Vanderbilt family into the upper crust of British nobility. However revenge was sweet, except for Willie K. and Consuelo's brothers, no Vanderbilt was invited to the ceremony.

Willie K. briefly increased his involvement in the railroads after brother Cornelius II, who had been extremely active, suffered a debilitating stroke in 1896. After Cornelius' death in 1899, Willie K.'s interest in the railroads waned, and he bought an estate in France and began breeding race horses.

Willie K. spent most of his time in France with his horses, and just before he died in 1920, he was the richest Vanderbilt alive. He died at age seventy-one, an intelligent, gentle man with no high purpose or direction in his life.

Yet, he still had loads of money. Even though he gave away $17 million in the last few months before his death (including $15 million to daughter Consuelo), he left a $55 million estate. His two sons Willie K. and Harold Stirling, each received $21 million.

It is not entirely clear why Cornelius II so greatly abhorred the marriage of his son **Cornelius Vanderbilt III** to Grace Wilson.

Grace Wilson was the daughter of a prominent southern railroad baron. The Wilsons had later moved north to New York and established a significant social reputation.

Grace was three years older than Neily, and had an earlier but fleeting fling with his younger brother. She also had been engaged to an English nobleman.

Maybe Cornelius could sense a certain shallowness or cold conceit in Grace, for she certainly cultivated a persona that would have repulsed the old puritan had he lived long enough.

The Vanderbilt family put on a full court press to scotch the marriage. But in the end, a headstrong Neily, after much anguish, married Grace anyway.

Grace Wilson Vanderbilt had a sweet tooth for high style, and the higher the better. Not that most other Vanderbilts didn't, but Grace's haughtiness and single-minded devotion to her role in the high caste were of an order of magnitude greater than most of her contemporaries.

Like many other socialites, she was enamored of Europe and its royalty. She traveled extensively on the continent and competed intensely for

Grace Wilson Vanderbilt

royal attendance at her affairs.

She aspired to and attained the highest level of social leadership. In her Newport cottage, Beaulieu and her Fifth Avenue mansion, she had probably the longest reign of anyone as queen of American society. It was estimated that in her heyday she entertained as many as 37,000 guests in one year.

Although there was some overlap of time, she didn't compete continuously with either Mrs. Astor or the Great Triumverate, for her halcyon years were mostly after their's.

Grace reeked of self-importance and pomposity and had no use for social climbers, those who sought to attain what she had as a birthright.

Grace was a great friend of Alice Roosevelt Longworth, a noted raconteur and the daughter of president Teddy Roosevelt. Alice caused considerable controversy when, while Grace's house guest, she danced the "hootchy- kootchy" on the roof of Beaulieu.

The Beaulieu estate, which adjoins Alva Vanderbilt Belmont's Marble House, was the setting for several sumptuous balls. Possibly the most famous was the *Fete des Roses*, a lavish production that transplanted an entire Broadway cast and set to the shores of Newport. The affair was so overwhelming that party guest Grand Duke Boris of Russia exclaimed "Is this really America or have I landed on some enchanted isle? Such an outpouring of riches! It is like walking on gold."

In his book, Grace's son recalls that night in the summer of 1902 when she stood on the lawn welcoming her guests "standing in a little green circle of light, looking like a portrait by Gainsborough in her ... pale-green and white gown and huge plumed black picture hat. With the costume she wore her cabochon emeralds and diamond stomacher. Directly behind her on the lawn of Beaulieu stretched a midway some 275 feet long, enclosed in turkey-red calico and blazing with red calcium lights looking, as one guest observed, like a 'tunnel of fire.' At the entrance to the midway stood a large jar of orchids and a Persian rug. Glowing fairy lamps and big baskets of red roses were scattered copiously throughout the estate. Gold and silver fireworks sprayed over the cliffs and the moonlit ocean."

Scores of carpenters and craftsmen built a wooden theater on the lawn for a one-night stand of the Broadway hit, *Red Rose Inn*. The entire cast (including stars Irene Bentley and Eddie Foy), scenery, lights, props, and stage crew were brought in from New York. The theater on Broadway closed for two nights.

Confirming its exclusivity, only one hundred couples were included in the rarefied air of this enchanted evening. After the play, dinner lead to dancing (two orchestras) into the wee hours, and the whole affair was capped by a sunrise breakfast.

Cornelius III (Neily) was the antithesis of Grace, and one wonders what they saw in each other.

Neily was frail, sickly and introspective, in sharp contrast to Grace, the overbearing and regal socialite. His sharp facial features were exaggerated by a pointy goatee.

Neily, after being cut out his father's will, developed a career with the family railroads. He became a prominent locomotive designer and engineer. Although he worked at the Vanderbilt railroads, he was not involved in senior management and had little contact with his estranged family.

He was an avid yachtsman, owning one of the most luxurious yachts afloat, the steam yacht *North Star*, and he became a Commodore of the New York Yacht Club. Possibly to escape from Grace and her social whirl, he joined the New York National Guard and fought in the Mexican War and World War I, rising to the rank of Brigadier General.

Grace traveled extensively in Europe, giving parties everywhere. Most of the trips were without Neily, and as their incompatibility increased, they gradually drifted apart.

Grace was relentless in her pursuit of social dominance. Her parties were known as the most lavish around, and everywhere she went she was the most richly dressed. Jewelry abounded, often including a dog collar of pearls high around her neck and a large diamond dangling from a rope of pearls and cascading across her bosom.

Between Newport and Fifth Avenue, the Vanderbilts entertained nearly every dignitary and big-wig around, from General Pershing to the Prince of Siam. This continued year-in and year-out as Grace marshaled an army of servants and a seemingly infinite bankroll to lock up the title of society's queen. In this process she managed to deplete an enormous portion of the Vanderbilt fortune.

Her social secretary met with her each morning to plan the details of future extravaganzas. She never saw any visitor who didn't have a pedigree as long as Fifth Avenue.

Grace and Neily's Newport mansion, Beaulieu was built in 1859 for the Peruvian ambassador Frederick de Barreda. Later it was owned by William Waldorf Astor who eventually sold it to Neily.

The cottage sits along Cliff Walk, overlooking the ocean. It is a massive but charming brick mansion. The house rises in perfect symmetry above a spacious terrace and is capped by a high concave French roof. The mansion gives the impression of dignity and power but in a much more understated manner than the giant stone palaces and castles of Bellevue Avenue and Ochre Point.

The likes of Grace Wilson Vanderbilt would have been better suited to the sumptuous Marble House or the Breakers, but Neily's net worth, although formidable, was nowhere near the magnitude of Willie K.'s or the late Cornelius II's.

Nevertheless, Grace made it clear that her summer cottage was as significant and resplendent as anyone's. To do this she employed a French chef, an English butler, and assorted maids, nursemaids, and footmen. She maintained seventeen different vehicles and thirty horses, along with fifteen stable boys and a coachman. The children were left to an English governess while Grace entertained and was entertained.

The Vanderbilt's English butler, Stanley Hudson was an imposing figure in the Beaulieu household. He changed his outfit three times a day and, except for his black vest, he was dressed just like Mr. Vanderbilt in the evening.

Next to the mistress and master, the butler held the highest rank in the household. And a good English butler could play this role to perfection. Hudson never opened the front door or answered the telephone; footmen would do this. He wouldn't set the table, serve meals, pour wine, or wash dishes; footmen, again. Hudson did greet guests, and speaking in the third person, he would say "If Madame will please be seated I shall see if Madam is in."

Grace's penchant for parties sometimes backfired. On one occasion, indignant Beaulieu servants staged a mild mutiny when Grace entertained the German ambassador at the outset of World War I.

It was the summer of 1914, Newport's last great social season, and the German army was rolling into Europe. Although the United States was not yet directly involved, there was heavy anti-German sentiment, particularly among the servant corps which was profusely populated by French, English, and Belgians.

But Grace had such a strong affinity for European royalty, and she greatly admired the Germans. So early in the summer she planned a huge August celebration for the dashing German ambassador to Washington, Count Bernstorff.

Neily, who at the time was a lieutenant colonel in the New York National Guard, was outraged. He railed at the idea and scolded Grace severely: "She ought to be ashamed to be entertaining the German ambassador when her many French and English friends were engaged in such a terrible war and her two English nephews were in front line trenches."

But even in the face of this stiff opposition, Grace was steadfast, the party would proceed.

After all, hadn't she had entertained the Kaiser's brother in 1902 at her Fifth Avenue mansion, and hadn't she feted the Kaiser himself in 1903 aboard the Vanderbilt yacht *North Star* in the Bay of Naples? No, the party would proceed.

So Cornelius Vanderbilt summarily announced that he would exclude himself from any affair honoring the Prussian Count.

Despite the obvious indelicacy of the situation and the uneasiness of all the guests, the Count appeared on schedule and sat down to a tense dinner. With the Count seated at the place of honor on her right side, Grace presided over an uneventful first course. After the footmen served soup in white Sevres plates bordered in blue and gold, they left for the kitchen to get the fish course.

When the fish failed to arrive on time, Grace dispatched her butler to the kitchen to ascertain the cause of this breach in schedule.

When the butler didn't return, Grace grew increasingly tense. Now they were way behind, and Grace was a stickler for the schedule. An eight course dinner better be served in an hour flat or the servants would risk her wrath.

After several minutes, a kitchenmaid of a neutral nationality (probably Irish or Swiss) apprehensively appeared with a note on a silver tray. It was from the insubordinate servants: "We the undersigned regret to inform you, Madam, that we cannot any longer serve the enemy of our respective countries. We have thrown the rest of the dinner into the dustbin and we have all left your service. There is nothing else to eat in the house. We hope you all enjoyed the soup, for we took good care to spit well into it, every one of us, before it went to the table."

The queasy guests reeled from the table after Grace read the message aloud. But after a brief recovery, the guests decided to prepare their own meal, and greatly enjoyed themselves amid the ensuing festival atmosphere.

Consistent with Newport's cachet, the servants returned the next day, and nothing further was mentioned by employer or employee.

Several other colorful Vanderbilts were closely connected to the Newport scene.

Alfred Gwynne Vanderbilt, Cornelius III's (Neily's) brother, benefited from Cornelius II's animosity toward Neily and inherited the bulk of their father's fortune.

Alfred's interests were diverse and encompassed nearly all gentlemanly pursuits, particularly horses and motorcars. He owned the vast Oakland Farm outside Newport and was an avid horseman. At Oakland Farm he built the largest exercise ring in the United States.

Alfred was the most handsome in this fourth generation of Vanderbilts. Slender with pleasing features, he had the look of a movie star.

Alfred and Neily never fully bridged the rift between them. They would merely nod and rarely speak when they met on Bellevue Avenue or at the Reading Room.

Alfred's first wife Elsie French Vanderbilt divorced him in 1908 on charges of adultery. She accused him of sexual misconduct with the wife of a Cuban diplomat while aboard his private railroad car, the Wayfarer. The testimony of Alfred's valet was key to the settlement which awarded Elsie French $10 million and custody of their son. The wife of the diplomat later committed suicide.

Alfred later married Bromo Seltzer heiress, Margaret Emerson McKim. They had two sons, Alfred Gwynne II and George Washington III.

In 1915, Alfred and nearly 1,200 others went down with the British liner *Lusitania* after a German submarine shot two torpedoes into her hull. There were several accounts of Vanderbilt's heroism in those last moments.

Alfred's estate exceeded $26 million. His first son, fourteen-year-old William Henry III (who became governor of Rhode Island), received Oakland Farm, along with a $5 million trust fund.

Mrs. Reginald Vanderbilt (Cathleen Neilson) in 1913 deserted by her husband.

Reginald Claypoole Vanderbilt was the younger brother of Neily and Alfred. Reggie owned another Newport farm called Sandy Point.

Reggie was rotund and had a round, rather homely face.

Reggie may not have had Vanderbilt looks, but he inherited more than a proportional share of Vanderbilt traits. He loved horses, gambling, wine, fast cars, and fast women.

After a disappointing stint at Yale, Reggie married Cathleen Neilson, a beautiful

Newport heiress.

Reggie distinguished himself with a series of gambling debts, automobile accidents, and other unsavory acts of hard drinking and debauchery. In 1915, Reggie was fined for cheating on his income taxes.

In 1912, he deserted Cathleen and their daughter while on a trip to Paris. He left them high and dry with no money and no explanation. Eventually Cathleen sued for divorce.

Reggie gambled extensively at Richard Canfield's casinos in New York and Newport (Canfield's Newport gambling house is now a prominent restaurant, The Canfield House). When police raided the New York casino they found $300,000 in I.O.U.s from Reggie.

Except for a $500,000 largess from brother Alfred's will, Reggie's cash flowed in one direction only, and by the early 1920s, high-living Reginald Vanderbilt had depleted a vast portion of his inheritance.

In 1923, Reggie married seventeen-year-old Gloria Morgan, the daughter of a prominent diplomat.

Alice-of-the-Breakers (Reggie's mother) was so fond of Gloria that one evening when they were dining she ordered a scissors and, snipping off a third of her $200,000 string of pearls, she handed them to Gloria. "All Vanderbilt women have pearls," she said.

For two wild years, Reggie and Gloria celebrated the Roaring Twenties. Between speakeasies, horse shows, and European trips they had a baby, whom they named Gloria.

Then Reggie's lifestyle caught up with him, and he suffered a series of physical breakdowns. On doctor's orders he swore off drinking and went to Vichy for the cure. But the day he arrived back at Sandy Point Farm, Reggie went to the Reading Room and promptly got drunk.

Two weeks later, Reggie suffered severe internal hemorrhaging and died. After debts were settled, Reggie's estate consisted of nothing except his original $5 million trust fund.

His daughter Gloria was the center of a bitter custody battle that raged well into the 1940s. It pitted mother Gloria Morgan against aunt Gertrude Vanderbilt Whitney. Little Gloria had three husbands including conductor Leopold Stokowski.

In 1899, **William K. Vanderbilt II**, the great grandson of the Commodore, was probably the most eligible bachelor in the country. Fresh out of Harvard, Willie K. II was a dapper dark-haired sophisticate and the paradigm of the young adventurous millionaire.

But in 1899 he was a man in love, in love with Virginia (Birdie) Fair of Rosecliff, the heiress to a large portion of the Comstock Lode. Although several years older than Willie K. II, Birdie was a vigorous and athletic young woman. A wedding was set for April.

The marriage melded two powerful families, and was masterminded by Alva Vanderbilt Belmont and Tessie Oelrichs, Birdie's older sister. Willie K II's father, the original William K. Vanderbilt, genuinely approved of the match even though his ex-wife was the matchmaker.

In the fall of 1899, the newlyweds took an extensive and hair-raising automobile trip through France. It was the early days of motoring, and conditions could be wild and woolly. They suffered several breakdowns and run-ins with the local culture as they careened through the countryside. The experience prompted Willie K. II to write what may have been the first guide for touring France by car.

The couple later purchased a villa in Newport and divided their time between New York, Europe, and Newport. Willie's $21 million inheritance assured a life free from the burdens of work and financial problems.

In Newport, Willie spent a lot of time racing around in his autos. He was even fined for speeding along Ridge Road. Also, he's credited with saving fellow cottager Foxhall Keene after a canoeing accident off Bailey's Beach.

Throughout his life, Willie was heavily absorbed in adventurous hobbies. He was a complete automobile aficionado. He and Birdie took several motoring trips through Europe. Willie delved into auto racing and even set records. He participated in the grueling 1903 Paris to Madrid auto race. Officials finally stopped the race after fifteen contestants were killed. In those days racing was primitive with few safety precautions.

Like many Vanderbilt families, Willie and Birdie separated, (in 1910), and were eventually divorced.

Willie had little interest in Newport social life and later devoted much of his time to his huge Long Island estate.

After Automobiles, Willie immersed himself in yachting. This wasn't just gentleman cruising, but heavy sailing on the high seas for extended periods. Willie explored the world and collected fish and assorted sea life for a museum he established at his Long Island retreat, Centerport.

When Willie died in 1944, his estate was valued at $36 million. This was before the age of aggressive tax planning, and the state and federal governments took $30 million.

Willie K. II's younger brother, **Harold Stirling (Mike) Vanderbilt** was quieter and less flamboyant, but no less the sportsman. Mike had the handsome and proud look of a Vanderbilt, and was by far the family's most famous yachtsman.

Willie K. Senior, Frederick, and Cornelius III had financed and syndicated previous America's Cup defenses, but none had actually sailed in the revered event.

Mike Vanderbilt successfully defended the America's cup three times when he skippered his victorious J-Boats off the coast of Newport. In 1934, he performed masterfully aboard *Rainbow* when his decision-making prowess overcame a 2-0 deficit and a technically superior British boat, the *Endeavor*. In 1937, realizing the existing defenders would be no match for *Endeavor II*, he single-handedly financed *Ranger*, an outstanding boat.

Mike helped frame the rules for contract bridge and invented a bidding system called the Vanderbilt Club.

In 1954, as a member of the New York Central Board of Directors, Mike witnessed the demise of Vanderbilt control over their railroad empire. In a bitter proxy battle for control of the railroad, Texas oil money prevailed over New York bankers. And Clint Murchinson, Sid Richardson and Robert Young (also of Newport) seized control of the corner office.

Mike and the rest were out; it was the end of an era.

THE DUKES OF NEWPORT

Doris Duke was called the "richest little girl in the world," when she was born in 1912. Doris was the sole heir to James Buchanan Duke's $100 million fortune, amassed primarily through tobacco (American Tobacco Co, et al.) and hydroelectric electric power (Duke Power Co.). As a tobacco baron, Duke built his fortune by gobbling up competitors and monopolizing the tobacco industry. Listed as the ninth richest man in the United States in 1913, "Buck" Duke was a gruff bear of a man who ruthlessly built up his multi-national tobacco trust. Duke, his wife Nanaline, and their only child Doris lived in a Fifth Avenue mansion, a fashionable London townhouse, a Colonial revival mansion in Charlotte North Carolina, an elaborate feudal estate in New Jersey and a Bellevue Avenue Newport mansion called Rough Point.

Eccentric and enigmatic Doris was pampered and sheltered by her doting father and grew up in a very strange household eventually becoming estranged from her mother. An insecure child with an overbearing and aloof mother, Doris was isolated and insulated from real life.

After renting "The Orchard" on Narragansett Avenue and later "Inchiquin" on Bellevue Avenue for several seasons, the Dukes finally won social acceptance and purchased "Rough Point" (the Frederick Vanderbilt mansion) from the widowed Nancy Leeds. Situated at the bottom of Bellevue Avenue and above the rocks on Cliff Walk the Gothic mansion commands a spectacular ocean view.

Rough Point

The Dukes kept a comparatively low profile in Newport. Buck Duke wasn't interested in society, and Nanaline entertained occasionally, albeit elaborately. Doris started her career as a recluse early. She liked to be alone and wasn't interested in golf, tennis, or socializing at Bailey's Beach.

In 1924, Buck Duke announced a stunning $40 million grant for health and education in North Carolina. This included $6 million for Trinity College in Durham. However, the endowment specified that Trinity change its name to Duke University. The board of trustees unanimously agreed to accept to offer. Buck commissioned architect Horace Trumbauer (The Elms) and the Olmsted landscape firm to design a new campus.

In the same year, Buck Duke established the Doris Duke Trust which bequeathed the bulk of his entire estate to Doris, with one third payable on her 21st, 25th, and 30th birthdays.

In late 1925, a few weeks after collapsing in Newport and being whisked to New York in his private railroad car, the *Doris*, Buck Duke died of pneumonia. On his deathbed the man who "created a nation of cigarette smokers" endowed Duke University with another $7 million and warned his daughter to "trust no one." His estate was worth an estimated $300 million.

With her doting father gone, Doris faced a life with an aloof and increasingly strict mother. Nanaline resented her daughter's wealth and power. Doris had all the assets while her mother had a lifetime income of $100,000 a year plus a life interest in the houses. At age fourteen, Doris successfully sued her mother and the other executors to prevent the auction of most of the real estate.

Doris' nonconformity increased during her teenage years. She created a stir when she took her maid swimming with her at Bailey's Beach. She shocked the old ladies at Bailey's when she bathed in an unlined transparent swimsuit. The heiress was constantly dogged by reporters; everything she did was news. In school, "the richest girl in the world" was a victim of resentment and jealously from classmates.

Nanaline set about scouting for Doris' future husband. A titled heir would be a good match for Doris and her trust fund estimated at half a billion dollars. She wintered in Palm Beach and summered in Newport, Southampton, or Bar Harbor, so her social exposure was great. In 1929, Evalyn Walsh McLean (Hope diamond) introduced Doris to the dapper "golden boy" Jimmy Cromwell, son of the wealthy Philadelphian, Eva Stotesbury. They invited Doris to Wingwood, the Stotesbury's fifty-room mansion in Bar Harbor. Jimmy was sixteen years older than Doris and a reputed playboy, who had recently divorced auto heiress Delphine Dodge and lost millions in a Florida land bust. During the visit, Jimmy unsuccessfully attempted to seduce the inexperienced sixteen year old by sneaking into her bedroom and slipping under the sheets. After the bungled tryst Jimmy pursued Doris sporadically for six years much to Nanaline's chagrin. The Stotesbury fortune like many others took a severe hit in the stock market crash and increased Jimmy's incentive to find a rich wife. The Duke investments weathered the crash relatively unscathed.

Rather tall at five feet eight inches, Doris wasn't a stunning beauty and didn't dress in the latest fashions, but she had a sleek, angular body that was classic 1930s chic. She had penetrating nearly Oriental sloe-eyed "tiger" eyes. Doris made her social debut at Rough Point during the summer of 1930. The current financial climate was an excuse for the penny-pinching Nanaline to cut party costs. So, the party, which was already competing with Robert Goelet's Ochre Court ball the same night, was not the elaborate affair many expected. It was dwarfed by social competitor and Woolworth heiress Barbara Hutton's Ritz-Carlton debut later that year.

After her debut, renegade Doris frequented Harlem jazz clubs rather than the chic dinner parties her mother would have liked. Aloof and self-conscious about her lanky looks, Doris still socialized often with Barbara Hutton. One socialite described encountering "Dee Dee" in one bedroom with a man and then catching "Babs" in bed with another man across the hall.

Like her mother, Doris developed a reputation as a skinflint, and was known as a poor tipper. According to one acquaintance she even rolled up her

Doris Duke

68

hair in toilet paper to save money on bobby pins. Doris' choice in men tended to be on the quirky, artistic, or wild side.

A kidnapping scare gripped social Newport in the early 1930s, and armed guards were often seen accompanying the Duke heiress to Bailey's Beach. In 1934, Jimmy Cromwell, whose fortune was fast disappearing, was invited to Rough Point. He and Doris were often seen at Bailey's Beach that summer. Doris knew that no one approved of Jimmy, but this made him more attractive to her. Also, Doris was anxious to get away from her mother; so, they were married in 1935. After a disastrous two-year honeymoon, characterized by fights and sexual incompatibility the couple built a huge estate on Hawaii. The ever eccentric Doris became an avid and accomplished surfer. The relationship suffered from extramarital affairs on both sides.

In 1940, Doris had well publicized affair with British M.P., Alec Cunningham-Reid and soon afterward her marriage to Jimmy ended in a bitter public divorce battle. Doris eventually won the case, but as a result of the ensuing scandal she was dropped from the New York Social Register.

Independent again and worth over $300 million at age twenty-eight, Doris became enamored of Hollywood and had a brief fling with Errol Flynn.

During World War II, Doris spent time in Europe as a war correspondent and excitement hunter. She reportedly spent several days with general George Patton, who was flush with victory after one of his most brilliant campaigns. After the war, Doris had a torrid European affair with Dominican Republic playboy, Porfirio Rubirosa. A tumultuous and brief marriage ensued.

In 1946, Doris returned to Newport to visit her estranged mother at Rough Point. At this time, Nanaline was meticulously managing Rough Point. She closely supervised the formidable gardening and floral operation which included constant rotation of dozens of flowers and potted plants. During the summer, the flower beds always bloomed. Varieties were rotated and changed when their color peaked. Servants policed the petunia beds early each morning, culling any dead flowers before Nanaline appeared.

The Rough Point staff was run ragged to constantly meet the Dukes' ever-changing demands. Stephanie Mansfield's biography of Doris Duke, *The Richest Girl in the World* quotes the son of the estate manager describing how "they would never give somebody a fifty-cent raise, but would spend a fortune on flowers without thinking about it." He commented on how "everything was worn for a minute and then thrown away" and how "everything was replaced and changed all the time." He describes the servants' precarious status: "they had no insurance or benefits. You were fired in a minute. You could work on the estate for thirty years and if you made a mistake, you could be fired on a Friday and left with nothing."

By the early 1950s, Doris' fortune had grown substantially, and her personal largesse also increased and included several jazz musicians. She was infatuated with jazz and had a long love affair with piano player Joey Castro.

Despite her paranoia (she thought everyone was trying to cheat her), Doris often invested in oddball schemes like treasure hunts or raising 25,000 deodorized pigs. She bought Falcon's Lair, the Hollywood mansion of Rudolph Valentino. Doris' other properties included the New Jersey family estate and Shangri-la, an ornate near-eastern style compound in Hawaii.

In 1954, Doris was outraged and hurt when rival Barbara Hutton married former flame, Porfirio Rubirosa. "Rubi" was Barbara's fifth husband. However, Rubi soon resumed an affair with Zsa Zsa Gabor and the marriage lasted only seventy-three days.

Doris was not warmly embraced by common Newport. The recluse would whisk in and out of town in her black limousine with darkened windows. She even tried to block the passage along Cliff Walk to prevent tourists from looking into Rough Point. However, access along the walk was protected by the Rhode Island constitution.

By the mid 1960s, Doris Duke had reportedly doubled her father's inheritance and was earning investment income of $1 million per week.

In 1966, Doris decided to renovate Rough Point back to its former splendor. She engaged interior decorator Eduardo Tirella her confidante and current "close" companion to assist in the restoration project. Tirella was a sophisticated and talented homosexual whose looks greatly attracted Doris.

In a tragic "accident," Doris crushed Tirella under her car as he was opening the gates to Rough Point. She reportedly hit the gas instead of the brake, and the car surged into and over Tirella. It was rumored that Tirella was tired of Doris possessiveness and temper tantrums and was about to leave her despite her heavy protests. A cursory investigation ensued, and Doris was not criminally charged in a very suspicious incident. Accident reports are missing from the Newport police station.

As time passed, Doris' penny-pinching paranoia worsened. She drove a beat up car. She would add up all of her bills even the minor ones to make sure she wasn't being cheated. She continued to treat employees like dirt and insisted they accomplish Herculean tasks in a short amount of time. Servants were docked pay if they broke glasses or caused other accidental damage. Her multiple household staffs were lucky to have a day's notice before her arrival. This resulted in a mad scramble to ready the estate. Potted plants and a myriad of flowers were hastily shuttled from greenhouses to their appointed places. Her guard dogs became infamous for terrorizing neighbors and passersby. Groups of German Shepherds and Dobermans continually patrolled Rough Point and her other estates both inside and out.

By the late 1960s, Doris' eccentricity continued to evolve. In addition to her penchant for jazz, Doris once traveled incognito with a group of black gospel singers. She was a friend of Albert Einstein and Elvis Presley. Despite her paranoia, she was constantly taken in by various con men, psychics, and gurus, and getting involved in hare-brained schemes involving seaweed or cosmic rays.

To Doris Duke's immense credit, she founded the Newport Restoration Foundation in the late 1960s. Doris' foundation initially bought forty-seven dilapidated but historic houses in Newport's "Point" section. The houses were meticulously restored to their colonial splendor and rented unfurnished to tenants. Doris enlisted the help of Jackie Onassis as first vice-president of the foundation. The houses were stripped to their foundations and rebuilt with new materials. Doris' mercurial personality figured heavily in foundation operations. She was demanding about all restoration details. Doris inspected all houses when they were finished, and she would think nothing of ordering a newly built fireplace and chimney torn down and moved a few inches. Tenants were generally regarded as serfs, and she issued strict rules on what they were allowed to do (which wasn't much). She had several run-ins with tenants. A big donnybrook erupted when she retroactively billed tenants for storm windows she had installed years earlier.

The foundation eventually restored nearly a hundred houses in addition to Prescott Farm in Portsmouth and Queen Anne Square in front of Trinity Church. In 1976, when Queen Elizabeth came to dedicate Queen Anne Square, Doris snubbed an invitation to dine aboard the royal yacht with President Ford, Henry Kissinger, and Elliot Richardson.

In the 1970s and 1980s, Doris' eccentricities and paranoia worsened. The Duke German shepherds were given the run of Rough Point. They would lie on the museum quality furniture and urinate on the expensive Oriental rugs and the servants were forbidden to reprimand them. In the early 1980s, Doris acquired Italian playboy Franco Rosselini as her latest "companion."

Her taste in food included a ban on all fat, lots of ginseng tea, and no white flour or refined sugar. She drank pure well water and never drank cola. However, she would have no problem consuming large quantities of wine. It was reported that for a time she went on an all-sardine diet. Doris never gave or threw food away. It could rot in the refrigerator for months.

At age seventy, Doris was swimming in her bikini off the precarious rocks of Rough Point. She was greatly involved in the paranormal and frequently had psychics and gurus as houseguests.

The Rough Point mansion was haphazardly dotted with priceless objects, such as boxes of diamonds. Doris even had a "pain machine," a twenty-foot long contraption that supposedly relieved pain by passing an electrical charge through the occupant. She even traveled to Switzerland for injections of sheep placenta, and she constantly took enemas to keep her girlish figure. She maintained a continuous animal menagerie, consisting mostly of dogs and birds.

Doris once had an inventory taken of all her personal property and it totaled more than one million items including numerous expensive art objects bought at auctions.

Doris Duke was a firm supporter of Claus von Bulow when he was charged and convicted of attempting to murder his wife Sunny. Doris came to von Bulow's birthday party in 1982. She claimed Sunny was an addict and that von Bulow was only a hapless participant in the tragedy.

She would order her staff to do all sorts of outrageous things like repaint all the patio chairs just before a luncheon or move her bathtub from New York to Hawaii. Often employees were ordered to stop what they were doing and catch the next plane to California, or Hawaii or...She even made the staff sign "loyalty" and confidentiality promises.

Doris' paranoia extended to air travel. She made reservations at the last minute often under a false name and would even buy an whole row of seats to avoid other people.

She was so cheap in most things but spent freely and gladly when it came to her animals. She once purchased $10,000 worth of azaleas only to have them all eaten by deer at her New Jersey farm. She didn't flinch at this, but if a servant threw away a bruised peach she'd have a fit.

In 1988, Doris acquired two camels ("Baby" and "Princess") for Rough Point. Often the camels were given the run of the estate, even the mansion. Servants had to clean up after them while like "bulls in a china shop" they wandered through the rooms.

Also in 1988, the seventy-five year old Doris adopted Chandi Hefner, a thirty-five year old hippie she met in Hawaii. The two women had been intimate companions for several years, and with time Chandi had assumed more and more of Doris' duties. The relationship gradually deteriorated as Chandi assertiveness and bizarre behavior increased. She alienated most of the staff. In 1991, after repeated heated arguments, Doris threw Chandi out and disinherited her.

Doris developed a close relationship with Imelda Marcos. The two soul-mates shared many common desires, like power, money, and the paranormal. Doris helped support Ferdinand and Imelda in Hawaii when their money was frozen and they were exiled. She also posted a $5.3 million bond for Imelda when she was arraigned in New York

In 1993, Doris Duke died at age eighty of cardiac arrest related to pulmonary disease. She left a fortune in excess of $1 billion. Doris left the bulk of her fortune to the Doris Duke Charitable Foundation. Most of the money was earmarked for support of performing arts, environmental work, animal care, children, and medical research. The will specified that Rough Point and Shangri-La in Hawaii be opened as public museums. She left $5 million to Bernard Lafferty, her butler and co-exectutor. She also provided "generous" gifts and forgave debts to her closest friends and employees. But she didn't forgive a $5 million loan made to Imelda Marcos.

The will also specified that Chandi Hefner was to receive nothing. The will was challenged by several parties, and it has been alleged that Doris death was "facilitated" by Lafferty the butler. In 1995, Lafferty was accused of squandering estate funds. He was seen at several parties sporting a ten-carat diamond earring, diamond shirt studs, and Doris' own forty-carat canary diamond ring. The issues were tied up in court for several years.

Eventually the estate was settled, with all the principals receiving something. Lafferty agreed to step down as executor. He died shortly afterwards.

Doris Duke truly had everything money could buy. But she was ultimately a sad case, someone with enormous power who freely broke the rules. Her wealth and personality combined to make her life radically different from everyone else. Severely insecure, money couldn't buy her what she probably really wanted, which was talent, beauty, and true friendship.

THE von BULOW AFFAIR

The story of Sunny and Claus von Bulow is a modern tragedy. They were in many respects the archetype "jet set" couple. She was a beautiful and wealthy Newport heiress, and he was a handsome sophisticate with an upper class European pedigree. They lived in Clarendon Court an exquisite Bellevue Avenue mansion and a luxurious Fifth Avenue apartment. They seemingly had it all. Today, Sunny lies in an irreversible coma, and Claus while a free man is branded by many as an attempted murderer. Their family is torn apart as a result of two bitter trials. The true story has been the subject of endless speculation, and the truth probably will never be known.

However, one version reads like this: a suave gigolo twice attempts to murder his wife, a wealthy Newport utility heiress, so he could get her fortune and marry his mistress. The plan is thwarted by the maid and stepchildren, and the husband is convicted and sentenced to thirty years in prison. A hotshot Harvard lawyer appeals the case, gets a new trial and the husband wins his freedom.

Clarendon Court

The media coverage of the televised trials was extensive. Several books and articles appeared, and actor Jeremy Irons won an Academy Award for his portrayal of Claus von Bulow in the movie *Reversal of Fortune*.

Both trials exhibited twists, turns, strange characters and bungled strategy, and until the O.J. Simpson trial, the von Bulow trials were perhaps the most closely followed by the American public in recent history.

Martha (Sunny) Crawford was the heiress to the bulk of the Columbia Gas and Electric fortune. She and her mother, Annie Laurie, both owned mansions in Newport: Clarendon Court and Champs Soliel, respectively. Clarendon Court is an elegant oceanside Bellevue Avenue mansion near Marble House and Rough Point. Sunny was a meticulous, shy, and self conscious woman. In 1957 She married an Austrian prince who didn't believe fidelity was part of marriage. The marriage ended in divorce after two children (Alexander and Ala).

In the late 1960s, Sunny married Claus von Bulow a shadowy figure who had no substantial resources. However, this polished Dane managed to win Sunny. They had one child, Cosima.

Sunny and Claus

Claus was gregarious and enjoyed society and all its trappings, while Sunny was uncomfortable in most social situations. Claus was tall (about six feet four inches) and thin with a somber expression. Sunny was beautiful blonde with a slim attractive figure.

Through the early 1970s, the couple grew gradually estranged. Claus wanted more freedom to pursue a career in corporate finance, but Sunny wanted a closely knit family life and a domesticated husband who stayed home. Claus claimed that Sunny lost interest in sex after Cosima was born.

The rest of the convoluted story depends on who you believe, and the arguments are strong for both sides

The step-children and the maid's side - Claus was a fortune hunting low-life scoundrel who plotted the destruction of his naive wife so he could marry a glamorous actress and expand his social ambitions. He injected a lethal dose of insulin after inaccurately portraying his wife as a troubled addict who contemplated suicide.

Claus' side - Sunny was a depressed drug and alcohol user who contemplated suicide. She injected herself with a lethal dose of insulin. The stepchildren and maid tried to frame Claus since they believed him guilty anyway but were afraid he'd get off.

Some facts are not in dispute. Sunny did fall into two comas. Both comas occurred at Clarendon Court around Christmas time, about one year apart.

COMA #1 - December 26, 1979 - Sunny went to bed early after drinking eggnog with her son Alexander. He noticed her slurred and barely audible speech. The next day Sunny lied in bed in an apparent stupor, while Claus read beside her claiming that she was just sleeping off a drinking episode. Eventually, after Sunny's maid became alarmed at her deteriorating state and insisted on a doctor, Claus summoned a doctor. As the doctor arrived, Sunny went into cardiac arrest. She was revived, taken to Newport Hospital and tested. She recovered.

COMA #2 - December 20, 1980 - After watching the movie *Nine to Five* at the Jane Pickens Theater, the family came home and Sunny talked with her children in the Clarendon Court library while Claus went off to make a business call. Once again Alexander noticed that she had slurred speech and appeared weak. Alexander helped his wavering mother to bed. The next morning Claus found her lying on the bathroom floor unconscious and in what turned out to be an irreversible coma.

His accusers maintained that Claus had the motive, means and opportunity to kill his wife.

THE MOTIVE - Claus stood to inherit $14 million if Sunny died. If Claus divorced Sunny, he would have only about $1 million. Claus' girlfriend, Alexandra Isles didn't want to be Claus' mistress, so she insisted he give up Sunny.

THE MEANS - Claus' black bag which was alleged to contain barbiturates, insulin and a syringe encrusted with insulin.

THE OPPORTUNITY - Von Bulow could have injected Sunny on the night of the comas. In the past he had injected her with vitamins. He could have pretended the insulin was a vitamin injection.

In the first trial Sunny's maid, Maria Schrallhammer was a key witness claiming that she had seen insulin and a syringe in von Bulow's "black bag." She also testified to von Bulow's "unhusbandly" behavior during the days of both comas. The stepchildren's testimony supported the maid. They hired New York attorney (Richard Kuh) to gather evidence; evidence that would have been excluded if gathered by the police.

The first trial in Newport ended in conviction for von Bulow as a strong prosecution with compelling evidence overwhelmed an inept defense. However, the conviction was overturned on appeal, and von Bulow was acquitted at a new trial. Harvard law professor Alan Dershowitz masterminded the aggressive appeal and uncovered much new evidence that undermined the prosecution's case.

The second trial had all sorts of colorful characters such as a bizarre self-proclaimed drug courier (David Marriott) and his friend, a Catholic priest (Philip Magaldi) of questionable background. Evidence was presented that Sunny was a drug user and even familiar with insulin injection as a means of weight loss. Sunny's friend, Truman Capote just before his death submitted an affidavit supporting these contentions. The defense established some doubt that the prosecution's insulin test was valid and that the encrusted needle was used to inject her. They also introduced Kuh's notes of an early interview with the stepchildren and maid, which made no mention of insulin. Much of the evidence related to the means and the opportunity was attacked vigorously at the second trial, and in the jury's mind reasonable doubt was established. Evidence related to the motive was suppressed at the second trial.

While Sunny no doubt had several psychological problems, there is some dispute as to their nature (low self esteem, depression, and alcoholism among others). Von Bulow in claiming his innocence maintained that she was heavily involved with drugs and alcohol, and he implied that she probably injected herself with insulin or some other drug. Newport society differs sharply on this issue. Doris Duke and Ann Brown were among Claus' most outspoken supporters. But the majority of Newport society was against him. Cosima believed her father, while Alexander and Ala actively worked toward Claus' conviction.

It appeared that Sunny's irreversible coma was caused by too much insulin. But if so, how did she get the insulin? Here are several of the most popular theories.
1. Von Bulow injected it under the guise of other medication.

2. Sunny injected herself either as an attempt to control her weight or to commit suicide.

3. Stepson Alexander was also a drug user and gave Sunny the insulin and then attempted to frame von Bulow.

4. Thinking that Claus must be guilty, the step-children and maid fabricated evidence to make sure he got convicted.

There was much more detailed evidence and controversy on both sides, such as alleged corruption in the Rhode Island legal system, von Bulow's frequenting of a prostitute, the egos of Alan Dershowitz, Herald Price Fahringer (von Bulow's first lawyer), Attorney General Arlene Violet and others. David Marriott proved to be a completely unreliable witness for either side and didn't testify. Father Magaldi was indicted for perjury and seemed to have an unusual relationship with Marriott.

After his acquittal, Von Bulow eventually came to a financial settlement with the stepchildren that reversed Cosima's disinheritance from her grandmother. Sunny continues her coma, and Claus is reportedly in England with a new girlfriend.

Two very different but fascinating books on the subject are *the von Bulow Affair* (by William Wright) and *Reversal of Fortune* (by Alan Dershowitz).

THE JAMES BOYS ET AL.

Before the Gilded Age really got rolling, there was a period when a large group of distinguished intellectuals flowered in Newport. This period was between the Southern planter era (pre Civil War) and the advent of the Gilded Age. Known as "Cottage Society," this group built elegant Victorian houses mostly in the Kay Street, Catherine Street, and the Old Beach Road section near Redwood library. Newport became the unique gathering place for artists, authors, and intellectuals of all stripes. Some maintained permanent residences while others visited for the summer. Notables like Oliver Wendell Holmes, Edgar Allen Poe, Bret Harte, John Singer Sargent, Clarence King, Alexander Agassiz, John LaFarge, Edith Wharton, and Henry and William James joined in this grand mix.

THE JAMES BOYS

Henry (1843-1916) and William (1842-1910) James, two of the most remarkable intellectuals of the American Renaissance spent many of their formative years in Newport. The James boys resided in Newport from 1858 to 1859 (at 64 Kay Street) and from 1861 to 1864 (at the corner of Spring

The James Boys

79

Street and Lee Avenue). Both boys were teenagers during most of this period. Their father, Henry James, Sr., a noted writer and theologian, shuttled the family around Europe and often back to the United States, constantly searching for the right educational environment for the children.

Henry James was a towering literary figure whose works arguably changed the face of the modern novel. William James was a leading American philosopher and psychologist, a ceaseless mental adventurer and a master of literary style.

Artist John LaFarge was a close friend of both boys during their Newport years. The James boys (aspiring artists) and he worked frequently in William Morris Hunt's art studio. At Newport Henry suffered what he described as an "obscure hurt" which bothered him physically and mentally throughout his life. We don't know the actual cause, and some have speculated on castration, but it was probably an injured back. This happened when he was fighting a fire on Old Beach Road. The boys attended the Berkeley Institute (in the Masonic building) on Church Street. They studied Latin and literature, and Henry met his lifelong friend Thomas "Sargy" Perry (descendant of Oliver Hazard Perry). The two friends read together at Redwood Library and walked all over Aquidneck Island, visiting such places as the Lily Pond, Forty Steps, the Big Pond, Hanging Rocks, and Purgatory Chasm, where they would have long philosophical talks.

Henry James was a purist and pursuer of the pristine. He walked extensively around Aquidneck Island, and wrote an essay describing Newport of 1870 as a place where "circles of friends" make up society and "the landscape and light refines the ordinary." However, Henry returned to a much different Newport in the early 1900s, and wrote an essay decrying the Gilded Agers and their lifestyles. He called the mansions "White Elephants" and symbols of witlessness on the mystical landscape of Newport. Henry was a master storyteller and author of numerous novels, essays and plays. He was also a peripatetic traveler and spent much of his time in Europe, eventually becoming a British subject.

Although the James boys' grandfather was quite wealthy, William and Henry were merely "well to do." Henry had a small inheritance but managed to support a fairly lavish lifestlye through book royalties.

William James was a Harvard educated physician and one of the founders of modern pharmacological psychiatry. Most of his eclectic philosophy was developed against a background of constant ill health including bouts of serious depression. His book *The Varieties of Religious Experience* (1902) is a classic study of religious psychology. William coined the term "stream-of-consciousness."

Henry James was a close friend of novelist Edith Wharton. Although both lived in Newport, it was at different times.

In 1907, Henry James joined Wharton and her husband Edward on a memorable motor-car tour through France. Henry struck a friendship with Wharton in 1900, and they were close friends until his death.

In 1910, William James died of heart trouble at his home in Cambridge, Massachusetts. Henry James died of a stroke in 1916 while living in England.

EDITH WHARTON (1862-1937)

Edith Wharton was a prolific novelist (forty-seven books), Newport intellectual, and disciple of Henry James. At the turn of the century, she lived in Land's End, a spectacular seaside villa located at the south end of Cliff Walk on Ledge Road.

Land's End

She was an unlucky-at-love enigma, and an uppercrust New York aristocrat herself with many society friends, but she had contempt for the Gilded Agers and their norms. Wharton, who was a immense figure in twentieth century literature, lived in a sexless marriage and was a member of a group she despised. She saw fashionable society as lacking a sense of beauty and good taste, and in her writing she scorned and attacked Gilded Age society for the degrading effect it had on American culture. In her brilliant novel *The House of Mirth* (1905) she tears into New York/Newport society as a group of pleasure seekers who take something beautiful (Lily Bart, the heroine) and debase it. Even though she had no formal education, Wharton wrote classic tales of the travails of upperclass American women, and in 1921 she won the Pulitzer Prize for her novel, *The Age of Innocence* (which was made into an academy award winning movie).

Edith Wharton

Wharton came from an Old Line New York family, that spent lots of time in Newport and Europe. Before her marriage she lived on the Pen Craig estate (and was known as "Pussie" Jones of Pen Craig) across the street from her domineering mother. Edith was extremely shy, and as a result people often mistakenly perceived her as cold and haughty. Showing contempt for the standards of the time, she married an unlikely partner hn Edward "Teddy" Wharton, an impecunious non-intellectual thirteen years her senior with no trade or future. In Newport husband Teddy enjoyed many of the things Edith despised such as the Newport Country Club, the Casino, and Bailey's Beach. The couple travelled extensively. Their intimate life was a disaster but the marriage endured twenty-eight years, ending in divorce in 1913.

For her first book in 1897, she collaborated with architect Ogden Codman to write *The Decoration of Houses*, a guide to interior decorating for the super rich. Thereafter she wrote a book almost annually. In 1902, she left Newport and built a house in Lenox, Massachusetts ("The Mount"). Shortly afterwards, Teddy Wharton, who couldn't cope with her success, suffered a series mental breakdowns.

In 1907, at age forty-five when she woke up to her sexuality and self esteem, she had the misfortune to fall in love with Morton Fullerton, a charming but egotistical playboy who was involved with many women. Their passionate love affair lasted one year until Fullerton grew tired of the relationship. In 1913, after she finally divorced Teddy, she sold The Mount and went to France to live.

Wharton wrote novels from about 1902 until her death in 1937. She received the French Legion of Honor for her volunteer service during World War I. Edith Wharton came back to the United states for the last time in 1923 to receive an honorary doctorate from Yale.

JOHN LA FARGE - (1835-1910)

John LaFarge was the premier American stained glass artist and muralist. He and his family had several residences in Newport. The most prominent being the large Victorian at the northwest corner of Kay and Bull streets. The family also spent time at Paradise Farm in Middletown and at 10 Sunnyside Place in Newport.

LaFarge's parents were wealthy French aristocrats who emigrated to New York City, where his father became a shipping and real estate baron. When LaFarge was twenty-three his father died, and he inherited enough money to allow unfettered pursuit an artistic career. He started in oil painting, studying with the James boys in William Hunt's studio on Church Street in Newport. LaFarge married Newporter Margaret Mason "Margie" Perry, a descendent of Oliver Hazard Perry and sister of Henry James' good friend "Sargy" Perry.

A commission for the interior design of Boston's Trinity Church boosted his fledgling career in 1876. After this he shifted focus from oil painting to decorative art and received numerous important commissions for public buildings and churches. Cornelius Vanderbilt II gave LaFarge a lucrative commission to decorate two formal rooms of his Fifth Avenue mansion. Throughout his life, LaFarge was constantly in and out of financial problems, and his chaotic business affairs often resulted in lawsuits and family feuds. To a large extent he matched the stereotype of the enigmatic self-centered artist with no head for the practical.

John La Farge

LaFarge's personal life was a disaster, and he largely ignored his wife and family who lived in Newport while he lived in New York and Boston and even traveled to the south pacific islands with Henry Adams. He had a sporadic but long lasting affair with his assistant Mary Whitney.

LaFarge is best known for his stunning stained glass designs and murals. In 1910, after LaFarge suffered a mental breakdown, Margaret committed him to Butler Hospital in Providence. He soon contracted pernicious anemia, and died a pauper leaving an insolvent estate.

BARONS AND BARONIES

A Tour Guide

The domains of the Barons of Newport are largely intact today. Most are private residences, but several are open for public viewing. The streets of Newport are a living museum of a fabulous era, and the explorer is rewarded with a fascinating tour.

The houses of Newport's Colonial leaders and merchant princes are found mostly near the center of the city, in the Historic Hill and Point sections. And most of the intellectual elite who inhabited Newport in the 19th century lived in the stately shingle-style mansions located in the upper Bellevue Avenue and Kay Street areas. But the mansions and castles of the Gilded Age millionaires are scattered throughout lower Bellevue Avenue and Ochre Point, along Cliff Walk, and around Ocean Drive.

Unfortunately, many of these marvelous relics have been demolished. The residences of such Newport barons as Harry Lehr, J. P. Morgan, and Harry Payne Whitney no longer exist. But fortunately so many others still stand, that Newport is truly a unique preserve of American Heritage.

The best place to start a Gilded Age tour is on that most famous street, Bellevue Avenue.

A STROLL DOWN BELLEVUE

Refer to map on inside back cover

Lower Bellevue Avenue stretches southward from Memorial Boulevard toward the ocean, to the beginning of Ocean Drive. An explorer starting from the north end will pass the stately Newport Casino on the left and almost immediately encounter turn-of-the-century mansions.

The first is **Kingscote** (c. 1850), on the right side of the avenue just past the Bellevue Shopping Center. **William King** purchased Kingscote in 1863, after making his fortune in shipbuilding, real estate, and the China trade. However, shortly after buying the house, King went insane and spent his remaining years in a mental hospital. Control of the house passed to family members who named it "Kingscote" (King's cottage) and added an additional wing in 1882.

In 1895, the British ambassador to the United States rented Kingscote and used it as his summer residence. During this time, "summer embassies" were common in Newport. Cossack guards stood in front of Stone Villa, the Russian "summer embassy," just north of Kingscote.

Kingscote

Richard Upjohn, the founder of the American Institute of Architects, designed the original Kingscote, and McKim, Mead and White designed the 1882 addition. Upjohn is well known for his Gothic revival style and was responsible for several churches including Trinity in New York and Saint Mary's in Portsmouth, Rhode Island.

Gothic Revival Kingscote, with its asymmetrical and irregular exterior lines, trimmed gables and dormers, and frieze-bordered roof edges, presents a charming and romantic image. The Gothic windows, variety of external forms, and rich detail contribute to this picture. The best view of the house is from the weeping willow tree at the edge of the circular drive.

The interior contains many of the same Gothic Revival features found on the outside: arches, columns, intricate woodwork, and variety in the size and shape of the rooms. The most ornate and unusual room is the

Bellevue House

McKim, Mead and White dining room with mahogany paneling, cherrywood floor, Tiffany glass-tiled walls, and cork ceiling. In 1972, The Preservation Society of Newport County inherited Kingscote and opened it to the public.

Berkeley Villa (also known as Bellevue House) is diagonally across the avenue, at the corner with Bowery Street. This Colonial Revival mansion was built in 1910 for heiress **Martha Codman**. She later married singer and famous art collector, **Maxim Karolik**, who was thirty years her junior. Karolik, who grew up in Russia, claimed to have heard of only three American cities: Washington, New York, and Newport. He described his boyhood image: "I didn't know much about Washington and I thought there were Indians in New York, but I did know one thing–that American millionaires spent their summers in castles in Newport." The couple spent twenty happy years in this house.

Elmcourt

Elmcourt, built in 1853, is on the right side of Bellevue Avenue, opposite Berkeley Avenue. This Tuscan Revival villa was one of the first on the Avenue. The Duchess de Dino once lived here in the 1800s, but for most of the Gilded Age it was owned by Frank Work of New York.

Berkeley House (1884-1885), on the corner with Berkeley Avenue, is a brick Queen Anne-style cottage built by Stanford White for **Leroy King**.

The **Isaac Bell House** (a.k.a., Edna Villa) (1882-1883) is on the right, next to Elmcourt. Designed by McKim, Mead and White, this cottage with its sweeping porches and diverse shingle patterns is a fine example of "shingle style" architecture. **Isaac Bell** was a New York cotton baron and key investor in the transatlantic cable. Bell was married to Jeannette Bennett, the sister of James Gordon Bennett.

The **Baldwin House** is on the left (1877-1878). It's a huge Queen Anne Revival combining brick, clapboard, and shingles into a Tudor style, with timbered gables, a penetrating chimney, and extending piazzas. The spacious interior hall is richly paneled and vaulted.

The Elms

On the right side of Bellevue Avenue, just before Dixon Street, is a massive stone mansion called **The Elms**. In 1901, Philadelphia architect Horace Trumbauer designed The Elms for coal baron **Julius Berwind**. Trumbauer modeled The Elms after the Chateau d'Argenson, an 18th century classic French chateau. The lavish interior decoration is the work of the renowned House of Alavoine of Paris. *Nouveau riche* Berwind, the son of poor German immigrants, made his fortune through his own efforts. In 1874, Berwind with his three brothers established a coal mining company which later became the dominant supplier to the United States Merchant Marine and Navy. Coal fueled the Industrial Revolution, and at one point the Berwinds owned 260,000 acres of coal land.

Although Berwind lived and worked in New York, he became a weekend commuter during the summer season, sailing on the Fall River steamer to Newport on Fridays and returning to New York on Sunday evenings. A servant staff of twelve to sixteen cared for the Berwinds in their summer "cottage." Usually the Berwinds entertained on a comparatively small scale, but the ball to inaugurate the opening of The Elms was a lavish affair. It was probably the most spectacular party of the 1901 season, with extensive floral decorations, three orchestras, 125 couples, and pet monkeys running over the lawn.

Following the French classical style, symmetry, balance, and clarity are integral characteristics of The Elms. The interior is exquisitely adorned with elegant objects of art, lavish ornamentation on the walls and ceilings, authentic Louis XIV and XV furniture, and splendid paintings loaned by the Metropolitan Museum of Art.

The ornate ballroom with curved corners presents a pleasing, flowing image to the eye. The opposing mirrors are interesting with their endless mutual reflections. The fabulous grand staircase is made of white marble and limestone. The bedrooms are small in comparison to their European counterparts–reflective of their use only during a short summer season. The terrace, lawn, and sunken garden exhibit horticultural excellence in the variety of plantings and meticulous design. The servants were quartered in a hidden sixteen-room third story. Note the statuary placed along the roof line.

Berwind's sister Julia last occupied the house until she died in 1961. Then the Preservation Society of Newport County purchased The Elms and opened it as a museum, preserved for public viewing.

De la Salle

De la Salle (1882-1884), the **William Weld** mansion, is directly across the Avenue from The Elms. Famed architect, Dudley Newton, designed this granite Gothic-style castle.

On the left, after Dixon Street, is **Wayside** mansion, the residence of Gilded Age raconteur and chief competitor of Harry Lehr, **Elisha Dyer**. **White Lodge**, the home of **Lispenard Stewart**, is next in line. This elegant villa had a Nile-green ballroom and a beautifully paneled dining room ornamented with delicate Gothic scrolls.

New York lawyer Lispenard Stewart was the most sought after bachelor in Newport. Trim, courtly, and conceited, Stewart was the epitome of Gilded Age gallantry. However, Stewart met his match in the rich and beautiful Mrs. Henry O. Havemeyer, Jr. She created a tense scene at one of Alva Belmont's Marble House balls when, although escorted by him, she spent the entire evening gossiping with friends. Stewart maintained his cool but vowed never to talk to her again.

After White Lodge, one encounters the **C.C. Baldwin** house, inexplicably named Chateau-Nooga (1880-1881). Windows and timbers abound in this ornate structure which was also known as the "Chatter Box." A huge gable and smaller partner dominate the front.

Just off Bellevue Avenue, on the corner of Narragansett and Spring, is **Oakwood**, the former **DeLancy Astor Kane** estate. The great oak trees complemented a beautifully landscaped grounds and gardens.

Rockry Hall is on the right, at the corner at Narragansett Avenue. This stone and shingle Gothic villa was built in 1848 for **Albert Sumner**.

The **William Osgood House** (1887) is on the left, across Narragansett Avenue. This rough-cut granite house is now headquarters for the Preservation Society of Newport County.

Swanhurst is on the right side, on the corner with Webster Street. Scottish stonemason, Alexander McGregor, built this fascinating fortress. The fine masonry walls in this Tuscan Revival villa are entirely obscured by a layer of stucco. McGregor, who also designed Fort Adams, Perry Mill, and the Newport Artillery Building on Clarke Street, built Swanhurst in 1851 for Judge Swan. Swan's descendant, Sallie Whiting, gave the house to the Art Association of Newport, and for many years it was an important cultural center.

On each side of Hazard Avenue are two estates once belonging to the renowned Brown family, the benefactors of Brown University. First is the **Harold Brown Villa**, a Gothic house designed in 1894 by Dudley Newton. The English-style landscaping was by the famed Olmsted firm, the designers of New York's Central Park. The nearby mansion was owned by **John Carter Brown**. The rounded portico matches a similar roof line topped by a romantic cupola.

Chateau-sur-Mer sits on the opposite side of Bellevue Avenue, set way back. This formidable but picturesque granite castle was built in the Victorian style and sharply contrasts (and pre-dates) the more ornate Gilded Age palaces found in this area. Chateau-sur-Mer was the most substantial and impressive Newport "cottage" when it was built in 1852 (and enlarged in 1872). At one time the property line extended to the ocean, hence the name Chateau-sur-Mer which means "castle by the sea."

Chateau sur Mer

The ballroom was the first of significance in Newport. In 1857, the *fete champetre*, given by owner **William Wetmore**, attracted an estimated 2,500 guests. This event, which presaged the gala turn-of-century balls, was the entertainment "benchmark" for Newport after the Civil War.

For generations, the Wetmore family was a prominent part of Newport. William Wetmore got rich in the China trade, and his son, George Peabody Wetmore was a powerful Rhode Island politician (governor and United States Senator). The daughters of George Wetmore, Edith and Maude, were leading Newport socialites and philanthropists. Edith Wetmore along with Mrs. John Jacob Astor pioneered the game of women's tennis at the Newport Casino when they daringly wore white tennis shoes, black stockings, white silk blouses, and pleated skirts with bloomers. The outfits were topped with sailor hats, over double veils to protect delicate faces from the summer sun.

The atrium-like central hall is Chateau-sur-Mer's most striking feature, rising forty-five feet to a glass ceiling and skylight and surrounded by balconies on each floor. The Italian decorator, Frulini, designed much of the interior, such as the walnut library, finely carved in Renaissance style. The carvings in the Frulini dining room extol the sensual pleasures of eating and drinking in Bacchic (god of wine) tradition. Underneath the stairs, the painted Tree of Life rises three stories to a ceiling decorated with birds and a blue sky.

Outside, the irregular Victorian lines, high mansard roof and rough granite walls present a harsh, sharp appearance. The huge weeping beech across from the entrance, with branches touching the ground, gives an explorer the feeling of walking through a forest.

Vernon Court

Mrs. Richard Gambrill, an influential widowed socialite, reigned from the majestic **Vernon Court** (on the left, past Shepard Avenue). Designed for lavish entertainment, this French Provincial chateau was built in 1901 by architect Thomas Hastings, the designer of the New York Public Library. White stuccoed walls, heavily ornamented in terra-cotta, and an enormous multi-chimneyed roof are prominent features of this sophisticated structure. The grand formal grounds include a copy of Henry VIII's garden for Anne Boleyn.

At the turn of the century, Scottish multi-millionaire, **I. Townsend Burden** owned **Fairlawn** (1852), an Elizabethan estate built of brick and brownstone. Fairlawn is just past Ruggles Street on the left side. Mrs. Burden was the first socialite to invite fellow Baltimorean Harry Lehr to Newport, thus launching a most bizarre social career. In 1883, the estate was owned by Levi Morton, who was Vice President of the United States in the Benjamin Harrison administration and Governor of New York. Salve Regina

University now owns Fairlawn, and it's the home of the Pell Center for International Relations.

Rosecliff

A little further down the avenue, on the left, one encounters the exquisite **Rosecliff** mansion, the summer residence of **Mr. and Mrs. Hermann Oelrichs**. The firm of McKim, Mead and White designed Rosecliff after the Grand Trianon Palace built by Louis XIV in Versailles.

From 1851 to 1891, George Bancroft–noted diplomat, historian, horseman, and horticulturist–owned the land now occupied by Rosecliff. Bancroft was the founder of the U.S. Naval Academy and Ambassador to England and Prussia. He is credited with establishing the extensive rose beds for which the property is named.

In 1891, Theresa and Virginia Fair purchased the Rosecliff property for $140,000. Theresa and Virginia (affectionately known as Tessie and Birdie) were the daughters of James Fair, an Irish immigrant who made a fortune by striking the largest vein in the Comstock Lode (one of the largest gold and silver deposits ever discovered). Tessie built the existing Rosecliff mansion in 1900 and became one of the outstanding hostesses of Newport society (see **The Great Triumvirate**).

Rosecliff is H-shaped, with two partially enclosed terraces. The garden terrace, an 18th century French Court of Love, was patterned after one built for Marie Antoinette. The first floor, used for entertaining, is about twenty feet high, while the second floor (bedrooms) is only ten feet. The concealed third floor was used for servants' quarters. The exterior is covered with white terra cotta, a fired clay that looks like stone.

The intention was entertainment on a grand scale, as seen in the spacious first floor design. Rooms and doors are arranged to permit the smooth movement of many people. The most striking feature of the interior is the spectacular curving marble staircase, which gracefully flows in a heart-shaped pattern. Other notable features are the massive archway leading into the stair hall, and the walls and ceilings (particularly in the ballroom), which are extravagantly adorned with carved and molded plaster fashioned into rococo designs.

The south rose garden, restored in 1976, has paths paved with marble chips and contains 180 plants. In 1973, scenes for the movie The Great Gatsby were filmed at Rosecliff. The Preservation Society of Newport County operates Rosecliff and provides guided tours.

Sherwood, Pembroke Jones

In the rarefied air of the strictly closed Newport society, the **Pembroke Joneses** were successful social climbers from North Carolina. Jones was a rice baron who rapidly penetrated High Society, after relocating to New York. The social gatecrashers set up housekeeping in the magnificent **Sherwood** mansion (1904), located on the right side of the Avenue, opposite Rosecliff.

The Joneses overcame objections from Newport's Old Guard by throwing lavish Southern dinners and entertaining in a grand style. Mrs. Jones regularly earmarked $300,000 for entertainment at the beginning of each Newport season. For one party, they thought nothing of building an 85 by 40-foot completely enclosed outdoor ballroom and theater, decorated with floor-to-ceiling plate glass mirrors and 10,000 water lilies.

Contrary to the social norms of Newport society, Pembroke Jones was always ready with a hearty laugh, a ribald joke, or a pre-lunch mint julep. According to legend, the fabulously wealthy Palm Beach real estate and hotel baron, Henry Flagler, met the love of his life, Mary Lily Kenan, while visiting Sherwood. In Cinderella tradition, Mary Lily was a poor relative of the Joneses and a shy recluse who spent her days upstairs sewing, until discovered by Flagler. As Flagler's young wife, she would later inherit an enormous sum and go on to became a most powerful and influential woman.

Sherwood is an expansive Georgian mansion, with a huge columned portico and several similarities to the "White House."

Beechwood

Marble House

Beechwood is located on the left side, opposite Bancroft Avenue. Beechwood was the home of **Mrs. Caroline Astor**, the queen of Newport society (see **Mrs. Astor**). This charming stuccoed brick house, with its spacious piazzas and breathtaking ocean view, was built in 1852. Beechwood is open to the public.

Adjoining Beechwood, is **Marble House**, the magnificent **William K. Vanderbilt** mansion. Marble House is most famous for its former mistress, the indomitable **Alva Vanderbilt Belmont**, full-fledged member of the Great Triumvirate and one of the most powerful American women of her time. Both Marble House and Alva Belmont are described in detail elsewhere in this book (see **The Great Triumvirate** and **The Vanderbilts**).

In apparent contradiction to its sunny name, **Champ Soleil** hides amidst the trees, on the right side. **Mrs. Drexel Dahlgren**, of the Main Line Philadelphia Drexels, built this profusely landscaped French Provincial estate in 1929.

This elegant mansion has a steeply-pitched roof and smart symmetrical lines. Later, Sunny von Bulow's family, (the Aitkens) bought the estate.

The **Beaulieu** mansion stands next to Marble House, on the edge of the sea. Beaulieu, built in 1859 for the Peruvian ambassador to the United States, has seen more than its share of Gilded Age barons. No less than **James Gordon Bennett, William Waldorf Astor, General Cornelius Vanderbilt, and Grace Wilson Vanderbilt** made Beaulieu their summer residence. The haughty and overbearing Grace Vanderbilt threw legendary parties throughout her long stint at Beaulieu (see **The Vanderbilts**).

Beaulieu has a charming French concave (mansard style) roof, densely bricked walls, and a deep sea-side verandah.

Clarendon Court is next to Beaulieu. The architect of the Elms, Horace Trumbauer, designed this 18th-century English mansion in 1904. **Edward Knight**, an executive of the Pennsylvania Railroad, was the original owner, but Clarendon Court has seen several other barons, including **Maysie Rovensky**, whose son Philip Plant is remembered as the husband of actress Constance Bennett. It is alleged that Plant's lifestyle was responsible for the coining of the word "playboy." The Rovensky's bequeathed Rovensky Park– across the Avenue from the mansion.

However, the most well known owners of **Clarendon Court** were surely **Claus and Martha "Sunny" von Bulow**. Claus was twice tried for attempted murder of his wife, after she lapsed into an irreversible coma resulting from insulin injections. He was convicted and then acquitted on appeal. After a lawsuit by Sunny's children, Claus agreed to give up rights to Clarendon Court and her inheritance. (see the **von Bulow Affair**)

Adjoining Clarendon Court is **Miramar**, another Horace Trumbauer work. **Mrs. George Widener** of Philadelphia built Miramar in 1914. The mansion, set in extensive formal gardens, is a model of classical architecture and rigidity. In 1912, the year construction began on Miramar, Mr. Widener and his son perished on the *Titanic*. Later Mrs. Widener married noted explorer, **Dr. Alexander Hamilton Rice**.

Mrs. George Widener

Miramar

Balls at Miramar were legendary, particularly during Tennis Week. In the Newport tradition, they lasted all night, but Mrs. Rice would nap shortly after midnight and return just before breakfast to freshly greet the revelers.

Mrs. Widener was the donor of Harvard's Widener Library.

Opposite Miramar and a little further down the avenue is **Belcourt Castle**, the former home of **Oliver Hazard Perry Belmont** and his wife, **Alva Vanderbilt Belmont**. Perry Belmont built this castle (for about $3 million) in 1894, two years before he married the former Mrs. William K. Vanderbilt, the ex-mistress of Marble House. The new Mrs. Belmont was one of Newport's great hostesses, and Belcourt became the scene of many fabulous balls.

Oliver's father, August Belmont, established the family fortune in banking and later married the daughter of Commodore Matthew Perry, thus linking the Belmont fortune with the prestigious Newport naval family, the Perrys. August built one of the early Bellevue Avenue mansions, the now-demolished "By-the-Sea" located near Marine Avenue, next to Rosecliff.

The Belmonts entertained extensively. Belcourt guests included the Duke of Windsor and Kaiser Wilhelm. Even lunch could be lavish, and Mrs. Belmont was known to invite friends from nearby Bailey's Beach back to the castle for a midday buffet of lobster, ham, and turkey. The Belmont family loved horses. Perry Belmont couldn't bear to be too far from them, so his were lodged on the first floor of Belcourt. The Belmonts helped build Belmont Park horse track in New York.

97

Prolific mansion architect, Richard Morris Hunt designed Belcourt and supervised construction over a three-year period. This sixty-room castle, patterned after a Louis XIII hunting lodge at Versailles, contains the largest collection of 13th-century stained glass in America. Antiques and art treasures abound in this eclectic museum. Oriental rugs (over 100), exquisite Renaissance furniture and paintings, and all sorts of armor and urns adorn the castle. The interior design of the castle reflects French influence, particularly from the 16th century.

Belcourt Castle

The Grand Hall, guarded by two imposing Italian marble columns, contains innumerable Chinese art work and an 18th-century bronze statue of Apollo. Apollo appears again in the dining room, driving his sun chariot along the ceiling. There's also indirect lighting designed by Belmont's friend, Thomas Edison. The archetypal Gothic ballroom is an amalgamation of vaulting stained-glass windows and columns. The room contains an extensive armor collection, 15th-century German throne chairs, and a great fireplace that looks like a castle. Belcourt was built for endurance; the brick and granite exterior walls are forty-two inches thick, and the castle sits on a four-foot thick concrete block.

The Tinney family now owns Belcourt Castle, and they have opened this spectacular museum for public touring.

Mr. & Mrs. Ogden Mills

Ocean View, across from Belcourt, is a distinguished Mansard-roofed wooden house built in 1866. During the Gilded Age, it was the home of **Mr. and Mrs. Ogden Mills**. The Mills were Old Line aristocrats who entertained in a formal, stately fashion. Mrs. Mills claimed she could give a party for a hundred without calling in extra help. But she was much too self-important and strait-laced to gain popularity among the more hedonistic Gilded Agers. Ogden Mills was Secretary of the Treasury during the Hoover administration.

Just past Ocean View, Bellevue Avenue turns ninety degrees to the right. **Rough Point** (1890) is at the tip of this elbow. Protected by stone walls, the mansion sits on the edge of the cliffs, above the pounding surf. This sandstone Tudor mansion, with its great Gothic hall and vast lawns, was the home of the immensely wealthy financier, **Frederick Vanderbilt**, the grandson of the famous Commodore.

Later in the Gilded Age, **Mr. and Mrs. William Leeds** lived in Rough Point. The *noveau riche* Leedses (he was known as the Tinplate King) were initially shunned by the Old Guard of Newport society. But they later won the support of Alva Vanderbilt Belmont and secured their place at the pinnacle. The young, charming, and beautiful Mrs. Leeds was to preside over many lavish balls at Rough Point.

Mrs. William Leeds

Later, tobacco heiress and famous Newport restorer, **Doris Duke**, lived in Rough Point (see the **Dukes of Newport**).

Roselawn is on the inside of the elbow, opposite Rough Point. **Mrs. J.F. Pierson** lived in this "carpenter Gothic" villa, with its multi-gabled roof and spacious porches.

Also on the right side, on the corner of Ledge Road, is **Inchquin**, a rough-cut granite French renaissance villa.

The Waves

On the left, all the way down Ledge Road toward the ocean, are two fine cottages situated at the end of Cliff Walk. **Land's End** (1890) was the home of novelist and Newport intellectual, **Edith Wharton** (see the **James Boys et al.**). The three-story, sixteen room stuccoed cottage sits on the left side of the road next to Cliff Walk.

The Waves is on the other side. In 1927, architect John Russell Pope (Jefferson Memorial) built The Waves for himself. The rambling multi-gabled villa blends nicely with the surrounding rocks and ridges.

Beachmound

Beachmound is the last house on Bellevue Avenue. Built in 1897, for Pittsburgh's **Benjamin Thaw**, this Colonial Revival mansion has a huge pillared portico and a great view of Bailey's Beach.

A WALK ALONG THE CLIFFS

Cliff Walk begins (on the north) at Memorial Boulevard, near Easton's Beach (First Beach). A walk along the entire span will yield spectacular views of the crashing surf on one side and fabulous Gilded Age mansions on the other.

A southward walker will pass a few notable cottages before arriving at Narragansett Avenue and Forty Steps.

Cliff Lawn (now called Cliff Walk Manor), one of the first great houses built on the cliffs, is on Memorial Boulevard overlooking First Beach. Cliff Lawn was the home of **Winthrop Chanler** and was the site of a christening party in 1902 for Chanler's grandson, which was attended by his godfather **President Theodore Roosevelt**.

About a quarter of a mile down the winding walk, is **Hopedene**, a Colonial Revival cottage built in 1902 for Mrs. **E. H. G. Slater** of Providence.

A little further is **Fairlawn**, a vast Queen Anne cottage with ornately carved Gothic gables, built for **Mrs. William Gammell** in 1889. Later, rubber baron, **Harvey Firestone** lived here.

Southside

Southside, another Queen Anne cottage, is just past Narragansett Avenue and Forty Steps. Famous Gilded Age architects, McKim, Mead and White designed Southside (1882) for **Robert Goelet** of New York. This

Mrs. Robert Goulet

magnificent house is a fine example of shingle style construction. Intricately arranged shingles, upper-level galleries, a multi-chimneyed roof, and a broad piazza mark the exterior. The interior opens freely around a great hall fireplace.

In a storybook romance, Goelet's son, Robert married Elsie Whelen, one of the poor, but gorgeous Whelen twins. The willowy Elsie became a classic Newport belle–tall and dark with long flowing lines and the picture of grace in a ballroom. Gilded Age author, Blanche Oelrichs describes these Newport belles: " How beautifully they stood and moved...with their evening dresses caught up under their breasts, wearing fresh gardenias in their hair, their slim throats encircled by necklaces of emeralds and sapphires." Alas, the couple soon divorced, and Elsie married Henry Clews of The Rocks.

Ochre Court

The next summer cottage is the ornate **Ochre Court**, the former home of **Mr. and Mrs. Ogden Goelet**. Ochre Court is a fifty-room French chateau built in 1888 for Ogden Goelet, a wealthy New York real estate developer.

Author Blanche Oelrichs describes Goelet as a man who worked himself to death. She recalls seeing Goelet shuffling around the grounds of Ochre Court on the arm of his nurse. She was told Goelet could digest practically nothing but grapes. Mrs. Goelet, on the other hand, became a most pursued widow. Enormously rich, arrogant and calculating, she entertained lavishly and lived in gilded splendor behind the gates. Mrs. Goelet is remembered as the hostess who battled Mamie Fish in the Grand Duke War (see **The Great Triumvirate**).

Architect Richard Morris Hunt modeled Ochre Court after Edward VII's castle in Paris. The design exhibits rounded arches, balconies, high roofs, turrets, and tall chimneys. Other exterior features include sandstone carvings of gargoyles, griffins, and relaxing workmen. The south wall even has a sundial. On the grounds, you'll find a colorful oriental Dogwood and a Copper Beech tree.

The Great Hall in Ochre Court rises three stories and is surrounded by an ornate balconied gallery. The ceiling features a banquet out of Roman mythology, and the Caen stone walls exhibit a myriad of symbolic carvings including dolphins, salamanders, and cherubs. The medieval stained glass window on the street side beside the grand staircase shows God the Father, the Devil, and other religious symbolism.

In 1947, Goelet's son Robert donated the mansion to the Catholic Diocese of Providence, and it is now the administrative center for Salve Regina University.

Vinland

Vinland is next in line along the Walk. It's the former summer home of **Mrs. Hamilton McKown Twombly**, the last of the great Newport *grande dames*. Mrs. Twombly, the last grandchild of Commodore Cornelius Vanderbilt, presided over Vinland for more than fifty years, before she died in 1952 at the age of ninety-eight.

Vinland, built in 1883, is a brownstone Queen Anne villa with fifty rooms. The Boston architectural firm of Peabody and Stearns designed

Vinland. At one point, the estate had more than fifteen automobiles, all painted in Vanderbilt maroon.

Mrs. Twombly's sumptuous dinners included the finest French *haute cuisine*, and her French chef became wealthy enough to retire in his own Newport cottage.

When she rode cross-country in her Rolls Royce to attend her grandson's wedding, Mrs. Twombly dressed as a maid and sat in front with the chauffeur, while her maid rode in the back disguised as the dowager.

The Breakers

Adjoining Vinland is **The Breakers**, the most fabulous and massive of all Newport mansions. The Breakers was built in 1892 by Richard Morris Hunt for **Cornelius Vanderbilt II**. Both the mansion and its occupants are described in detail elsewhere in this book (see **The Vanderbilts**).

As Cliff Walk turns sharply to the right (west), **Anglesea** sits on the point with a commanding view of the ocean. It's a rambling stick-style cottage built around 1880. It has been recently renovated to a modern estate.

The walk continues around Ochre Point skirting **Fairholme**, enlarged in 1870 for **Fairman Rogers** from Philadelphia. Rogers was the author of the authoritative manual on coaching. This large Tudor villa, with medieval half-timbered facade, was later owned by the Drexel family. However, **Mr. and Mrs. Robert Young** were probably the most famous owners. Railroader Robert Young–of Newport, Palm Beach, and White Sulphur Springs–was the tycoon who wrested the reins of the New York Central from the Vanderbilt family. Mrs. Young, the sister of famed artist, Geor-

Fairholme

gia O'Keefe, often entertained the Duke and Duchess of Windsor at Fairholme.

A little further along the Walk is **Midcliff** (1886), the former home of Oklahoma oil heiress, Minister to Luxembourg, and hostess *par excellance*, **Pearl Mesta**. She entertained Dwight Eisenhower and Hoover's vice president, Charles Curtis.

Midcliff is followed by **Honeysuckle Lodge** (1886), a rambling Queen Anne cottage and former home of famous golf enthusiast, **T. Suffern Tailer**.

EXPLORING OCHRE POINT

After Honeysuckle Lodge (at Marine Avenue), Cliff Walk continues southward for more than a mile. The Walk gradually becomes more primitive and ends at Ledge Road. Most of the mansions along this section also border Bellevue Avenue and are described earlier. However, the oceanside perspective is rewarding and should not be missed.

There are several other mansions of interest in the general Ochre Point area (between Ochre Point Avenue and Bellevue Avenue).

Edson Bradley, a Washington D.C. liquor baron, built **Seaview Terrace** in the late 1920s. It's patterned after the French Renaissance style of a Norman manor house, with a soft-toned limestone exterior extensively adorned with cornerstones and cornices. The house is located on Ruggles Avenue near Cliff Walk, just west of Honeysuckle Lodge.

Mr. Bradley filled his house with tapestries, stained glass, and an eclec-

Seaview Terrace

tic selection of art treasures. This fifty-four room mansion was one of the last great houses built in Newport and contained a chapel which seated 150 people.

However, it wasn't completely built in Newport. It seems that Bradley had some sections removed from his Washington home and shipped by railroad to Newport, where they were reassembled.

Seaview was shown as the opening scene for the old television series, "Dark Shadows." The house is also known as the Carey Mansion and is used by Salve Regina University.

Watts Sherman House, c. 1900

The **Watts Sherman House**, located on Shepard Avenue near Lawrence Avenue, is a classic example of Queen Anne style. This Tudor manor house was built in 1874 for New York banker **William Watts Sherman**.

The Watts Sherman House, designed by H.H. Richardson (Boston's Trinity Church), was the premier American model and trendsetter for shingle-style architecture. The exterior, dominated by two enormous gables set at right angles, builds from a stone base into a rich texture of shingles arrayed in intricate patterns, small-paned bay windows, and half-timbering set in terra-cotta stucco. The interior has a spacious central hall with a great free-standing fireplace, exquisite paneling, ornate wood carvings, beamed ceilings, and La Farge stained glass.

In total, three renowned American architects had a hand in Watts Sherman. A later addition was designed by Dudley Newton, and Stanford White redecorated several rooms. The house is now a Salve Regina residence hall.

Wakehurst

At the corner of Lawrence Avenue and Bowery Street is **James Van Alen's** former home, **Wakehurst**. The mansion is a fascinating copy of an English country manor house. At first glance, it seems almost a mini Elizabethan castle, as it lords over a beautifully landscaped estate, but it's really a charming stone Tudor mansion. English architect, Charles Kempe, designed Wakehurst, patterning it after Wakehurst Place in England. Dudley Newton supervised the building process. The rooms were imported from England and reassembled in the mansion. The exterior is striking with its multiple gables, ball-topped pinnacles, diamond-paned window bands, and stone sculpturing.

Miss May Van Alen granddaughter of Mrs. Astor

Van Alen was a railroad heir who married Mrs. Caroline Astor's daughter, Emily. After his wife died, Van Alen hoped to become the Italian ambassador, but crusading Joseph Pulitzer, publisher of the New York World, who had no use for the idle-rich Van Alen, scotched the appointment by printing a scathing editorial against Van Alen's lifestyle.

James Van Alen, handsome and elegant, was Newport's most eligible widower. But maybe most of all, he was a consummate Anglophile. He loved everything British and adorned Wakehurst with English tapestries, antique "period furniture," high-backed oak benches, dower chests, grandfather clocks, pewter tankards, etc. Eccentrically, Van Alen even flavored his vocabulary with such Tudor period expressions as "egad," "zounds," "varlet," and "wench." Van Alen was firmly established at the upper crust of Newport society. He was a connoisseur of food and wine, and his musicales and parties were the height of fashion.

Wakehurst is now part of Salve Regina University.

Set behind the trees at the east end of Narragansett Avenue, opposite Ochre Point Avenue, is an elegant French chateau known as **The Orchard**. The mansion was built in 1871, and is an exact copy, formal grounds and all, of an 18th-century French country house. During the Gilded Age the house was owned by **Colonel George Fearing**.

Traveling west on Narragansett Avenue, an explorer will soon encounter **Bois Dore'**, one of the last great Newport mansions (1927). The design is decidedly 18th-century France for this huge limestone chateau built for Pennsylvania's **William Fahnestock**. Fahnestock was known for hanging 14-carat gold artificial fruit from the trees of the Bois Dore' estate. The property was later owned by oil heiress, Carolyn Skelly.

A RIDE AROUND THE DRIVE

The southern end of Bellevue Avenue is a good place to begin a tour of Ocean Drive. The Drive starts at Ocean Avenue, near Bailey's Beach, where Bellevue Avenue ends.

On the left, just past Bailey's Beach, is a stick-style cottage known as **The Ledges**. The rambling house, built in 1867 for **Robert Cushing**, has a commanding view of the ocean and the surrounding shoreline.

William Miller's French chateau sits on the opposite side, high above the shore. The stucco and timber facade has the look of a fortress against a hostile environment. Miller appropriately named his house **High Tide** (1900). Automobile baron, Joseph Frazier later owned the mansion.

Mrs. Stuyvesant Fish's Colonial mansion, Crossways (1898), was the scene of many famous social events. A member of Newport's Great Triumvirate, the outrageous Mamie Fish was one of the most colorful socialites of the Gilded Age (see **The Great Triumvirate**). The columned, colonial mansion is on the right, just before Gooseberry Beach.

Ocean Drive

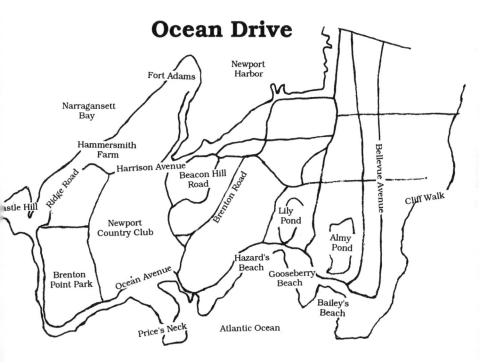

Idle Hour, a French provincial manor house is on the right side, opposite Hazard's Beach and overlooking Lily Pond. It was built in 1929 for **Colonel and Mrs. Fredric Allen**, who in 1931 hosted French Marshall, Henri Petain. Petain, a World War I hero and later Vichyite appeaser, came to Newport aboard a French cruiser to celebrate the 151st anniversary of the French troop landing in Newport. Idle Hour was later owned by Mrs. John Payson Adams, the former Muriel Vanderbilt.

On the left, past Hazard's Beach, is a series of magnificent oceanside cottages: **Nearsea** (1937), **Little Clifton Berley** (1930), **Eagle's Nest** (1924), **Normandie** (1914), **Seafair** (1937), **Bay House** (1917), **Play House** (1926), and **Wildacre** (1901). French and English architectural styles dominate this charming array of houses.

Normandie is the brick mansion behind the white wall, with an arched gatehouse entrance. Frederick Sterling, a United States ambassador to Sweden was a former owner. Wildacre was the home of **Albert Olmsted**; the Olmsted brothers were the premier landscape architects of the Gilded Age.

Opposite Wildacre, up on a bluff, is a stone and shingle mansion designed by Richard Morris Hunt in 1891. The secluded **Wrentham House** blends harmoniously with the surrounding rocks and shrubbery. It's now called Avalon and was recently the home of tennis pioneer, James van Alen.

Ocean Avenue winds past the venerable **Newport Country Club** (1894) on the right and around Brenton Point to Castle Hill.

Castle Hill

The **Castle Hill House** (now the Inn at Castle Hill) was the home of Professor **Alexander Agassiz**, the renowned marine scientist and turn-of-the-century intellectual. The shingle mansion (1874) has a great view of the East Passage of Narragansett Bay.

Ocean Avenue runs into Ridge Road, which winds back towards Newport Harbor. Past the Coast Guard station, on the left side, is **Shamrock Cliff** (now Ocean Cliff), the former **G. M. Hutton** estate. The main house (1896) is patterned after an Irish country castle.

Hammersmith Farm is near where Ridge Road turns into Harrison Avenue. In 1888, **John Auchincloss** built this twenty-eight room Victorian summer cottage. When John F. Kennedy married Mrs. Hugh Auchincloss' daughter, Jacqueline, the wedding reception was held at Hammersmith Farm. Later, President Kennedy made Hammersmith Farm a summer White House.

Hammersmith Farm

The shingle-style construction and the airy rooms are appropriate for this seaside cottage. The shingles wear well in the salty air flowing freely through the spacious rooms and terraces. The large deck room is lined with glass doors that open onto a flowered terrace. The grounds and gardens are beautiful, containing a wide variety of trees, shrubs, and flowers. A corridor of meticulously pruned silver linden trees is one of the highlights.

Just after Hammersmith, there's a small farmhouse near the entrance to Fort Adams. The farm was the setting for **Harriet Beecher Stowe's** novel, "The Minister's Wooing."

Beyond Fort Adams, overlooking Brenton Cove, is a classic Georgian mansion perched precariously on the rocks and looking like a Greek temple. McKim, Mead and White designed **Beacon Rock** in 1889 for **Edwin Morgan**. It was later owned by Felix de Weldon, sculptor of the Iwo Jima statue.

Edgehill, another McKim, Mead and White design, was built in 1887 for **George King**. The turreted stone and slate villa is on Harrison Avenue, before Beacon Hill Road.

At Edgehill, Harrison Avenue turns ninety degrees to the left and proceeds down to **Beachbound** (1895), a huge granite and shingle castle built by Peabody and Stearns for **William Burden**. The mansion is right on the water, with a great view of Newport Harbor.

Harrison Avenue turns sharply to the right and passes by **Bonniecrest** (1912-1918), a classic Tudor stone and brick manor house designed by John Russell Pope for **Stuart Duncan**. The landscaping was by the famed Olmsted brothers. Ironically, Bonniecrest, the scene of more than a few fabulous balls, resembles country manors in Worcestershire England, and Mr. Duncan was chairman of Lea and Perrins, makers of Worcestershire Sauce (see photo in **Of Mansions and Madness**).

Just past Bonniecrest, Harrison Avenue intersects Halidon Avenue, a short road leading down to the harbor. On the left, before the harbor and behind a stone wall, is **Harbour Court**, the former residence of **Mrs. John Nicholas Brown** of that famous Providence family. Harbour Court, built in 1904, is an enormous French chateau with a great view of Newport Harbor. The New York Yacht Club is the current owner.

Beacon Rock